THE ULTIMATE Chocolate COOKBOOK

THE ULTIMATE Chocolate COOKBOOK

JENNIE REEKIE

NEW YORK

Acknowledgements

Food photography   Peter Myers
Home economist   Jackie Burrow
Stylist   Alison Williams

The author and publisher would also like to thank The Glasshouse and
Way-In Living, Harrods for kindly loaning equipment for
photography.

First published in Great Britain in 1983
by Ward Lock Limited, 82 Gower Street,
London WC1E 6EQ, a Pentos Company.

First published in USA 1984
by Exeter Books
Distributed by Bookthrift
Exeter is a trademark of Simon & Schuster, Inc.
Bookthrift is a registered trademark of Simon & Schuster, Inc.
New York, New York

ISBN 0-671-06803-2

Printed and bound in Spain by Graficas Reunidas

Contents

NOTES

All spoon measures are level unless otherwise stated.
All eggs used are large unless otherwise stated.
Flour is sifted all-purpose unless otherwise stated.

Introduction

Few people would dispute that chocolate is the most popular sweet flavor in the Western world. Individual fruits, such as strawberries, raspberries and mangoes may have their devotees, and there may be some who are enslaved by the flavor of almonds or coffee; but nothing is as revered as chocolate. Strong men who spurn all other desserts go into raptures over a chocolate mousse or Black Forest Gâteau, while no self-respecting restaurant would offer less than three chocolate desserts on their sweet trolley.

For some people, their passion for chocolate verges on addiction; they crave for it in the same way that others desire a cigarette, but it is unlikely to be as harmful as smoking unless eaten to excess! There is however, no escaping the fact that chocolate is high in calories, and it must be said that this is not a book for the slimmer. But as well as large quantities of fat and carbohydrate, chocolate contains significant amounts of protein, iron and calcium. In fact, when cooking with chocolate, it is not always the chocolate that threatens the waistline, but the cream, sugar and flour that is used with it.

For the most part, chocolate cookery is not the cheapest, simply because the chocolate itself is expensive. It is probably because this basic ingredient is rather a luxury that one tends to use other luxurious ingredients with it such as nuts, fresh cream and alcohol. Chocolate has an affinity not only with rum and brandy, but also with a number of liqueurs including Grand Marnier, Tia Maria and crème de menthe and with those based on coconut.

The result is an array of wonderful concoctions from mousses and soufflés to moist rich cakes, gâteaux and petits fours, and I hope that in the following pages you will be tempted, not only by some of the tried and tested favorites, but by some different and original ways of using this ambrosial ingredient.

7

Choosing Chocolate for Cooking

There are three main types of chocolate commonly used in cooking – unsweetened, couverture and semisweet or bittersweet chocolate, of which unsweetened chocolate is the one most frequently used in this book. White chocolate is not suitable for cooking because it contains no cocoa and, therefore, of course, no color.

Unsweetened chocolate is chocolate especially prepared for cooking. It enables you to achieve a strong chocolate flavor without the end result being too sweet, but I have restricted its use here to just a couple of recipes as it is not very easy to obtain.

If you do find some, and want to experiment, try using it in one of your favorite recipes. It is particularly good in chocolate sauces or for baking – but remember to use slightly less of it than other chocolate and to add a little sugar.

Semisweet or bittersweet chocolate gives a good strong chocolate flavor. There are a number of different brands available; and some supermarkets have their own brands as well. Remember though that chocolate quality varies considerably. In order to be called chocolate, the product must have a minimum of 34 per cent cocoa solids. Some have as much as 47 per cent, so it is worth looking on the back of the package to check this.

As well as bars of chocolate, you can also buy packages of 'chips'. These have two particularly useful functions: they are good for melting chocolate because the small pieces melt quickly, and the size is perfect for ice creams and cookies.

Milk chocolate is rarely used in cooking as it does not give a strong enough chocolate flavor. This can sometimes be an advantage if, for example, you wish to grate a small amount of chocolate over fruit with a delicate flavor. It is, however, used for making Easter eggs, chocolates and chocolate cases, such as the Apricot Fruit Basket on page 72. Chocolate chips are probably the best thing to buy if milk chocolate is required for anything other than grating, as they are usually cheaper than bars.

Compound chocolate comes both sweetened and semisweet. It is not really chocolate because it does not have the required minimum of cocoa solids and contains added vegetable oil. It produces less flavor than semisweet chocolate, but has some advantages. It is cheaper and easier to melt than semisweet chocolate. It also avoids the streaky effect sometimes visible after melted semisweet chocolate has set.

Cocoa is certainly the cheapest, and often the best, way of obtaining a good, strong chocolate flavor, especially when baking. However, it is not used as extensively as unsweetened chocolate for desserts and mousses where a richer flavor is required.

Instant chocolate milk mix can be used to give a more subtle flavor, but as it is very sweet it is almost always necessary to reduce the amount of sugar in the recipe.

Chocolate Tips

MELTING CHOCOLATE

The way in which you melt chocolate is extremely important so as to avoid a solid mass with which you can do nothing.

Break the chocolate into pieces (or use chocolate chips) and put into a bowl over a pan of hot, not quite simmering, water (it must *not* be rapidly boiling). If using an electric cooker, turn off the heat once the water has boiled and leave the pan on the ring. Make sure that the bowl fits comfortably into the pan so that neither steam nor boiling water get into the bowl. As soon as the chocolate has melted, remove from the heat and use as required.

If, you do, however, end up with a solid mass, it is sometimes possible to rectify this by adding a little vegetable oil and beating it well. This works for mousses and similar desserts but not for decorations where it is important for the chocolate to set hard.

Chocolate can also be melted with the addition of vegetable shortening. This makes it more liquid and easier to handle.

If you are only melting a small quantity of chocolate, such as 1 ounce, you may find it easier to put the chocolate into a polythene bag, then to seal it and stand the bag in hot, *not* boiling, water. It is important to use a heavy gauge polythene and to ensure that there are no small holes in the bag.

Melting chocolate in a bowl in a slow oven is an alternative method recommended by some manufacturers.

A microwave oven can also be used for this purpose. Put the chocolate broken into pieces, in a suitable bowl, cover with clingfilm and place in the oven. The exact time it takes to melt the chocolate depends on the quantity, the size of the bowl etc.

PREPARING CHOCOLATE FOR DIPPING

When using chocolate for dipping, ie for fresh fruit or for chocolates, you may find the chocolate a little easier to use if you add 1 tablespoon vegetable oil or 1 tablespoon white vegetable shortening to every 6 ounces chocolate.

Melt the chocolate, then pour it into a small jar or glass wide and deep enough for the fruit or chocolate to be dipped into and totally covered.

Hold the ingredient to be dipped with a special dipping fork, fondue fork, skewer or toothpick. Dip into the melted chocolate, allow the excess to run off, then remove the dipped ingredient from its fork by pushing it off gently with another fork, skewer or toothpick.

MAKING 'BITTER' CHOCOLATE

As unsweetened chocolate is not easy to find, semisweet chocolate is generally substituted. Where this is a little too sweet for certain recipes, the chocolate can be made slightly 'bitter' by adding either 1 teaspoon instant coffee powder or granules, or a little very strong black coffee. Alternatively, 1 teaspoon cocoa powder can be added for every 2 ounces chocolate.

GRATING CHOCOLATE

During hot weather it is best to put the chocolate in a refrigerator for about 30 minutes before grating. If your hands are rather hot, hold the chocolate in a piece of paper toweling when grating.

CHOPPING CHOCOLATE

This can be done very successfully in a food processor and for many recipes this gives a very good size of chocolate chip. It is not, however, easy to chop chocolate manually, and it is better, in this case, to grate it coarsely.

USING COCOA AND INSTANT CHOCOLATE MILK MIX

When baking, sift cocoa and instant chocolate milk mix with other dry ingredients so that any lumps are removed.

If using cocoa in buttercream, etc, it is important to cook the starch in it, so it should be blended with *very hot* water. (Do not use boiling water as it tends to make a solid lump which is difficult to use).

OTHER POINTS

When using any kind of mold, ensure that it is scrupulously clean so that the chocolate does not stick to the mold and crack. Wash the mold thoroughly in warm water, then dry and polish with a piece of paper toweling.

Decorations

Chocolate can be used to make a variety of extremely attractive decorations. These can be used on all kinds of cakes, puddings and desserts, quite apart from chocolate ones. For example, cream-topped trifles and pale iced cakes make a perfect foil for the dark appeal of chocolate.

For most decorations the chocolate must be melted and the finished product allowed to set quite hard. This should not be done in a refrigerator or the chocolate will acquire an unattractive chalky 'bloom'. It is best to leave it in the coolest, driest place you have – I put mine, covered, in a shady corner of the back yard when the season permits (a kitchen is too warm and steamy to be suitable).

Grated chocolate is the simplest and quickest of decorations, and is very effective. Using a metal grater, and making sure that your hands are cool, grate the chocolate directly on to the food or, if you prefer, on to a plate from where it can be sprinkled with a metal spoon. Do not use your fingers to work with the grated chocolate as the fine particles will melt quickly.

Chocolate curls can be made from semisweet or couverture chocolate. Use a thick bar of chocolate – the thicker the bar the more successful the results – and make sure it is at the right temperature, ie if it is too cold and hard the chocolate will break; if it is too warm and soft the curls will not hold their shape. Simply scrape a vegetable peeler over the back of the bar of chocolate and roll the curls on to a plate. Lift them from the plate with the point of a sharp knife on to the surface to be decorated.

Caraque are long chocolate curls which give a professional and rather glamorous finish to many cakes and gâteaux. Melt the chocolate (page 10) and spread it with a spatula to less than ¼ inch thick over an ungreased surface, preferably a Formica counter or a marble slab. Leave to set in a thin layer. Holding the blade of a knife at an angle of 45°, push away from you and scrape off long curls. Lift them carefully, as they are fragile, using the point of the knife or a skewer; do not discard the small flakes of chocolate that remain on the working surface after you have finished; they can be scattered on top of the cake or dessert in between the pieces of caraque.

Chocolate leaves are made by using real fresh leaves as a mold. The most commonly used leaves are rose leaves because they have a pleasing shape, prominent veining which impresses itself on the chocolate and a glossy finish which makes them easy to work with. Any leaves will do, however, as long as they are not poisonous.

Wash and dry the leaves thoroughly. Dip the underside, which has the most prominent veins, into melted chocolate (page 10) to give a thick and even coating; alternatively, paint with the chocolate. Place on wax or non-stick silicon paper to set. Let the chocolate set completely hard, then carefully peel off the leaf.

Horns are made with the help of cream horn tubes. Wash and dry them and shine the inside of the tubes with absorbent paper. Pour in some melted chocolate (page 10). Tilt and turn the tube so that the chocolate coats the inside evenly; repeat the process to obtain a thicker layer of chocolate (this will be easier to unmold. As you become more proficient, you can make thinner horns.) Leave to set in a cool, dry place. When the chocolate is completely hard, and has begun to shrink away from the inside of the tube, carefully ease out the chocolate horn with the point of a knife.

Chocolate animals are also made by pouring melted chocolate (page 10) into molds; these are available from good gourmet shops and are the perfect decoration for children's party cakes.

Shapes, patterns and designs can be made in two ways:
(1) Pencil your chosen design lightly on a piece of wax or non-stick silicon paper. Melt the chocolate (page 10) and pour it into a pastry bag or nylon piping bag fitted with a small writing tip. Follow the outline of your drawing first, and fill in the shape afterwards. If you are not making a solid design, but are tracing a trelliswork pattern, for example, make sure that you join up all the threads of chocolate, or the finished design will crack easily when you pick it up after it has set.
(2) Melt the chocolate (page 10) and spread in a thin layer with a spatula on a piece of wax or non-stick silicon paper. Leave to set. When the chocolate is hard, but not brittle, use cookie cutters or a sharp knife to cut out the shapes you want. You can buy cutters in all shapes, from crescents, hearts and bells to butterflies and stars. Simple shapes like squares and triangles can, of course, be cut out with a sharp knife and a steady hand.

Drizzled chocolate is a simple but extremely effective method of decorating cakes, ice cream or cookies. Simply melt the chocolate in a polythene bag, snip off a corner of the bag and let the chocolate drip over the food to be decorated.

Making Chocolate Candies

What present could be more appreciated than a pretty box of home-made chocolate candies? The great thing is that they are fun to make, and generally much cheaper than bought ones. It is easy to make them look attractive in paper candy cases, arranged carefully in a box or jar and tied with ribbon. And to end your dinner party in style, impress your guests with a bowl of home-made chocolate-covered mints or delicious truffles.

All the recipes here are very straightforward, but once you have mastered them you are sure to go on and experiment with more complicated ideas. While no detailed confectionery knowledge is required, it is, nevertheless, necessary to know how to recognize the different temperatures used when boiling sugar (see chart below). If you progress to making fudge and toffee regularly, it is well worth investing in a candy thermometer as this is an easy and quick way of checking the temperature.

Sugar Boiling Temperatures

Temperatures	Candy Stage	Method of Testing
215–225°F	Thread	Dip the handles of two wooden spoons first into some oil and then into the boiling sugar syrup. The syrup should form into a fine thread when pulled apart.
240°F	Soft Ball	A little of the syrup can be rolled into a soft ball in your fingers when poured into a cup of cold water.
250°F	Hard Ball	The mixture forms a larger, harder ball than obtained with the Soft Ball test above.
280°F	Soft Crack	A few drops of the syrup poured into a bowl of cold water soon becomes brittle and a thin piece will snap.
310°F	Hard Crack	Test as for the Soft Crack, but the syrup becomes very brittle.
345°F	Caramel	The sugar changes to a pale golden-brown and the longer it is boiled, the darker it becomes.

Easter Eggs

Making Easter Eggs at home not only saves money, but provides amusement for all the family, especially for children who will not find it difficult, especially if you use compound chocolate.

Plastic and metal molds can be obtained from most good gourmet shops. Make sure they are dry and clean, and polish them well with a piece of paper toweling before you set to work. Do not grease the molds. Melt the chocolate (page 10) and spoon some into the mold, tilting it to coat the inside completely. If you have too much, pour it out before it sets; if you have too little, quickly spoon in some more.

Place the mold upside-down on a sheet of wax paper and leave it in a cold place to set (not a refrigerator). When the first layer of chocolate is hard, you can add another one; this will make the egg easier to unmold, but it is not vital.

When the chocolate is hard and has shrunk away from the edges of the mold a little, ease it out gently with a spatula.

Fill the Easter egg with candies and chocolates if you like, and join the two halves by brushing the rims with melted chocolate and pressing them gently together.

Note *Remember that any casualties which break when removed from the mold, can be re-melted and used again.*

Chocolate Dipped Fruits

These provide attractive, quickly made petits fours. A variety of different fruits is suitable, from strawberries and grapes to cherries, peeled lychees and mandarin sections. Choose ripe but firm fruit, free from any blemish. If the fruit has a stem, such as a cherry, leave it on. Make sure the fruit is clean and dry, and dip each one in melted chocolate (page 10), holding it by the stem if it has one, otherwise using a toothpick. Place on wax, or non-stick paper and leave in a cool place to dry. When the chocolate has set, put the dipped fruit in petits fours cases. Do not store for more than 24 hours; they are at their best up to 12 hours after the chocolate has set.

Rich Chocolate Truffles

4 ounces semisweet chocolate, broken into small pieces

1 tablespoon liqueur, eg Grand Marnier, Cointreau, Tia Maria, etc

2 cups confectioners sugar, sifted

½ cup unsalted butter

2 tablespoons instant chocolate milk mix

Melt the chocolate (page 10). Remove from the heat and beat in the liqueur, confectioners sugar and butter until smooth. If necessary, add a little more confectioners sugar to give a firm paste. Divide into 24 pieces and shape into balls. Roll each one in the instant chocolate milk mix until completely covered, then place in paper candy cases.

Makes 24

Chocolate Rum Truffles

4 ounces semisweet chocolate, broken into small pieces

1 tablespoon dark rum

2 tablespoons unsalted butter

1 egg yolk

1 cup ground almonds

1 cup cake crumbs

¼ cup chocolate **or** colored vermicelli

Melt the chocolate with the rum (page 10). Beat in the butter and egg yolk, then remove from the heat. Stir in the ground almonds and cake crumbs to make a smooth firm paste. Divide into 24 pieces and shape into balls. Roll in the vermicelli until completely covered, then place in paper candy cases.

Makes 24

Chocolate Cream Truffles

4 ounces milk chocolate, broken into pieces

4 tablespoons heavy cream

¼ teaspoon vanilla extract

2½ cups confectioners sugar, sifted

2 tablespoons extra confectioners sugar

¼ teaspoon ground cinnamon

Melt the chocolate (page 10), then stir in the cream and vanilla extract. Remove from the heat and gradually beat in 2½ cups of the confectioners sugar to give a firm paste. Divide into 24 pieces and shape into balls.

Sift the remaining confectioners sugar with the cinnamon on to a sheet of wax paper. Roll the truffles in the spiced sugar until completely coated, then place in paper candy cases.

Makes 24

ABOVE   Making chocolate leaves (page 13)
ABOVE RIGHT   Making chocolate horns
(page 13)
RIGHT   Making caraque (page 12)

Mint Crisps

4 tablespoons water

4 tablespoons granulated sugar

1 teaspoon peppermint extract

8 ounces semisweet chocolate, broken into small pieces

Well butter a piece of wax paper. Put the water and sugar into a small, heavy-based pan. Stir over low heat until the sugar has dissolved, then boil rapidly to 280°F on a candy thermometer (soft crack stage). Remove from the heat and stir in the extract. Pour evenly over the wax paper and leave to set. When the mixture is quite firm, either break up into small pieces with a rolling-pin or chop finely in a food processor; the pieces should resemble coarse breadcrumbs.

Melt the chocolate (page 10), then remove from the heat and stir in the peppermint pieces. Put teaspoonfuls of the mixture on sheets of buttered wax paper, spread into circles about 1 inch in diameter, and leave to set.

Makes about 30

Chocolate Peppermint Creams

The creams look particularly attractive in a box if half are green and half are white.

1 egg white

¼ teaspoon peppermint extract

a few drops green food coloring (optional)

3 cups confectioners sugar, sifted

4 ounces semisweet **or** milk chocolate, broken into small pieces

Put the egg white, extract and coloring, if used, in a mixing bowl and beat lightly. Beat in the confectioners sugar gradually to make a firm paste (the exact amount of sugar will depend on the size of the egg). Place on a surface lightly dusted with confectioners sugar and knead until smooth. Roll out, using confectioners sugar to prevent it from sticking, to a thickness of about ¼ inch. Stamp out circles, using a 1½ inch cutter and place on a cookie sheet lined with wax paper. Mark each one with the prongs of a fork. Leave in a warm place overnight to dry out.

Melt the chocolate (page 10). Dip each peppermint cream in the chocolate so that only half is coated. Shake off any excess chocolate and place on buttered wax paper or foil. Leave to set.

Makes about 48

A Selection of Candies
*Chocolate Dipped Fruit (page 15), Colettes (page 20), Chocolate Peppermint Creams, Walnut Mocha Fudge (page 23), Easter Eggs (page 15), Chocolate Cream Truffles (page 16) **and** Fruit and Nut Clusters (page 22)*

Colettes

8 ounces semisweet chocolate,
broken into small pieces

4 tablespoons water

1 tablespoon strong black coffee

1/4 cup butter

2 egg yolks

1 teaspoon dark rum

Melt 4 ounces of the chocolate (page 10). Remove from the heat and put a good teaspoonful into 18 waxed paper candy cases. Using the handle of a teaspoon, spread the chocolate evenly round the base and sides of each case. Leave to set in a cool place.

Put the remaining chocolate into a small pan with the water and coffee. Stir over very low heat until the chocolate has melted, then boil for 2 minutes, stirring frequently. Remove the pan from the heat and allow the mixture to cool. Beat in the butter, a little at a time, then blend in the egg yolks and the rum. Leave in a cold place until thickened.

When the chocolate cases have set, peel off the paper candy cases carefully. Spoon the filling into a pastry bag fitted with a 1/2 inch rose tip and pipe into each chocolate case.

Makes 18

Chocolate Whirls

A recipe producing very rich, smooth chocolates.

1/4 cup soft brown sugar

2 egg yolks

1/2 cup light cream

7 ounces semisweet chocolate, broken into small pieces

Put the sugar and egg yolks in a mixing bowl over a pan of hot, not boiling, water. Beat together until pale and thick. Blend in the cream and continue to cook, stirring until the custard coats the back of a spoon. Turn off the heat, but leave the bowl over the pan of water. Add the chocolate, and stir until it has melted. Cover and leave to cool until the mixture is of a piping consistency. Spoon into a pastry bag fitted with a large star tip and pipe in whirls into paper candy cases. Leave to set.

Makes 18

Note *If the mixture is allowed to set before being piped, it should be reheated over a pan of hot water.*

Stuffed Dates

These are quite deliciously rich, and, although you can make them with dried dates, they really are better made with fresh dates as these are not quite so sweet.
In addition to being served as chocolates or petit fours, these dates are also excellent dipped into whipped cream.

1 pound fresh dates
3 ounces semisweet chocolate, broken into small pieces
¼ cup butter
1 tablespoon ground almonds
1 egg yolk
*1 tablespoon Grand Marnier **or** other orange liqueur*
grated rind of 1 small orange

COATING
6 ounces semisweet chocolate, broken into small pieces
1 tablespoon vegetable shortening

Using a sharp knife, make a slit down the side of each date and remove the seed. Pull off the hard remains of the stem. Melt the chocolate (page 10) and remove from the heat. Cream the butter. Beat in the ground almonds, then the egg yolk. Beat in the Grand Marnier, orange rind and finally the chocolate. Mix well, then chill in a refrigerator for about 10 minutes, or until the mixture is firm enough to pipe.

Fill a small pastry bag fitted with a small plain tip about ¼ inch wide with the mixture, or put it into a heavy-gauge polythene bag, work it down to one corner and snip off the corner with shears. Holding the dates between the thumb and forefinger, press them open and pipe the filling into the center. Chill in a refrigerator for about 15 minutes.

To make the coating, melt the chocolate with the vegetable shortening (page 10), and pour into a narrow deep glass or cup. Taking one date at a time, skewer one end with a toothpick and dip into the melted chocolate. Allow the excess chocolate to drip off, then place on a piece of foil and use a second stick to push the date off the dipping stick. Leave to set.

Makes about 24

VARIATION *Fill the dates with half of the mixture and then pipe the remainder on to some buttered wax paper, making small 'blobs' the size of a large marble. Chill for about 15 minutes, then dip into melted chocolate and leave to set.*

Fruit and Nut Clusters

4 ounces semisweet chocolate,
broken into small pieces

4 tablespoons honey

½ cup mixed dried fruit

¼ cup nuts, chopped, eg almonds, hazelnuts
or brazils

grated rind of ½ orange

DECORATION
candied cherries

Melt the chocolate with the honey (page 10). Stir in the dried fruit, nuts and orange rind until well coated in the chocolate. Drop teaspoonfuls of the mixture on to buttered wax paper, or into paper candy cases. Press a small piece of candied cherry on the top of each cluster and leave to set.

Makes 24–28

VARIATION *Use milk chocolate instead of semisweet chocolate.*
Different colored candied cherries look very attractive.

Chocolate Toffee

2 cups granulated sugar

½ cup butter

½ cup water

¼ teaspoon cream of tartar
(optional)

4 ounces semisweet chocolate **or** compound
chocolate, broken into small pieces

Butter a shallow 7 inch square baking pan. Put the sugar, butter, water and cream of tartar, if using, in a large pan. Stir over low heat until the sugar has dissolved. Bring to the boil and cook without stirring to 280°F on a candy thermometer (soft crack stage). After 250°F is reached (hard ball stage), reduce the heat and cook very slowly up to the required temperature. Remove from the heat and add the chocolate. Stir gently until melted, then pour immediately into the prepared pan. When beginning to set, mark into squares with a sharp knife. Leave to set, and cut into squares when cold.

Makes 36

Note *These toffees can be wrapped individually in waxed papers for storing.*

Chocolate and Orange Fudge

This makes a soft, smooth, creamy fudge.

1 pound granulated sugar

½ cup milk

4 ounces compound chocolate,
broken into small pieces

½ cup butter

grated rind and juice of 1 orange

Well butter a shallow 7 inch square pan. Put all the ingredients in a large pan, and stir over low heat until the sugar has dissolved. Bring to the boil and boil rapidly to 240°F on a candy thermometer, (soft ball stage). Stir from time to time to prevent it from burning. Remove from the heat and leave to cool for about 3 minutes. Beat rapidly until thick and creamy. Pour immediately into the prepared pan. When it is beginning to set, mark the fudge into squares with a sharp knife. When cold, cut into squares.

Makes 36

Walnut Mocha Fudge

This makes a firm, crunchy fudge.

2 cups soft brown sugar

¾ cup canned evaporated milk

½ cup water

¼ cup butter

1 tablespoon instant coffee granules

4 ounces semisweet chocolate **or** compound chocolate, broken into small pieces

½ cup walnuts, chopped

Well butter a shallow 7 inch square pan. Put the sugar, milk, water, butter and coffee in a large pan. Stir over low heat until the sugar has dissolved. Bring to the boil and boil rapidly to 240°F on a candy thermometer (soft ball stage). Stir from time to time to prevent it from burning. Remove from the heat and stir in the chocolate until melted. Add the walnuts, and beat until the mixture is thick and creamy. Pour immediately into the prepared pan. When it is beginning to set, mark into squares with a sharp knife. When cold, cut into squares.

Makes 36

Large Cakes and Gâteaux

No matter whether they are plain, layer cakes, rich, moist dark cakes or gâteaux filled with thick whipped cream and fruit, chocolate cakes are supreme. Most are made with cocoa, some with instant chocolate milk mix and others with melted chocolate. The methods of making them are varied, too, which is why a chocolate cake is never just another cake – each one is quite different.

There is also a wide choice of fillings and toppings ranging between whipped cream, simple buttercream made with either cocoa or melted chocolate, rich Continental buttercreams, fudgy frostings and rich, thick glacé frostings. The possible variations are innumerable, and all of them mouthwatering.

A number of the gâteaux in this chapter could be served as a dessert rather than with morning coffee or afternoon tea. If you think I have omitted some of your favorites, look for it either in the Cold Desserts or Chocolate Classics chapters – I hope you'll find it there.

Simple Cake

This very easily made cake is perfect as a base for a children's birthday cake. Turn it into a maypole by putting a stick in the center with some streamers coming from it, or decorate it with candies spelling the child's name.

1¾ cups self-rising flour
¼ cup cocoa powder
a pinch of salt
1 cup caster sugar
½ cup butter **or** margarine
¾ cup canned evaporated milk
2 eggs
2 tablespoons water
1 teaspoon vanilla extract

FILLING AND TOPPING

2 cups confectioners sugar
¼ cup cocoa powder
⅓ cup butter

Grease and line two 7½–8 inch layer-cake pans. Sift together the flour, cocoa, salt and sugar into a large bowl. Melt the butter or margarine in a pan. Take 3 tablespoons of the evaporated milk and put into a small pan for the frosting. Put to one side. Beat the eggs with the remaining evaporated milk, water and vanilla extract. Make a well in the center of the dry ingredients, add the egg mixture together with the melted fat, and beat well until blended.

Divide the mixture between the prepared pans and bake in a medium oven, 350°F, for 20–25 minutes or until the cakes spring back when pressed lightly. Allow to cool in the pans for a few minutes, then turn out on to a wire rack and leave to cool.

To make the filling, sift the confectioners sugar and cocoa into a bowl. Put the butter into the pan with the reserved milk, and heat gently until the butter has melted. Pour over the confectioners sugar mixture and beat until well blended. Put to one side for about 10 minutes until the mixture begins to thicken. Use some of the mixture to sandwich the cakes together, and spread the remaining frosting over the top and sides. Decorate as liked.

Economical Chocolate Cake

This is an old war-time recipe of my mother's; it makes a very good, plain cake.

1/4 cup softened margarine

1/2 cup caster sugar

1 egg, beaten

1 1/2 cups flour

a pinch of salt

2 teaspoons baking soda

1 tablespoon cocoa powder

4 tablespoons milk

FROSTING

1/4 cup margarine

1 tablespoon cocoa powder

2 1/2 cups confectioners sugar, sifted

2 tablespoons hot water

Grease and line a 7 inch baking pan. Cream the margarine, add the sugar and continue to beat until the mixture is light and fluffy. Beat in the egg, a little at a time. Sift together the flour, salt, baking soda and cocoa and fold into the creamed mixture, alternately with the milk.

Turn the mixture into the prepared pan and bake in a medium oven, 350°F, for about 50 minutes, or until the top springs back when pressed lightly. Allow to cool in the pan for 5 minutes, then turn out on to a wire rack and leave to cool. When the cake is quite cold, split into two rounds.

To make the frosting, put the margarine and cocoa into a small pan over low heat until the margarine has melted. Remove from the heat and beat in about a third of the confectioners sugar, then beat in a little of the hot water and the remaining confectioners sugar alternately. Beat well until the mixture begins to thicken. Spread evenly over both rounds, and swirl the frosting up on the top of the cake with a round-bladed knife or fork to make an attractive pattern. Sandwich the rounds together. Leave to set for at least 15 minutes.

Note *It is particularly important that the margarine is very soft.*

Moist Chocolate Cake

A perfect recipe which time is of the essence. Once baked, this really good moist cake can be completed in minutes.

2½ cups soft brown sugar

¼ cup cocoa powder

½ cup water

2 cups flour

2 teaspoons baking soda

½ teaspoon bicarbonate of soda

½ teaspoon salt

½ cup butter

1 teaspoon vanilla extract

2 eggs, separated

½ cup sour cream

FILLING AND DECORATION

4 tablespoons chocolate and hazelnut spread

confectioners sugar

Grease and line two 8 inch layer-cake pans. Put ¾ cup of the sugar into a pan with the cocoa and water. Stir over low heat until the sugar has dissolved, then bring to the boil and simmer gently for 2 minutes. Remove from the heat and allow to cool. Sift together the flour with the baking soda, bicarbonate of soda and salt. Cream the remaining sugar and the butter until light and fluffy. Add the vanilla extract and beat in the egg yolks, one at a time. Fold in the dry ingredients alternately with, first, the cooled chocolate and then the sour cream. Beat the egg whites until stiff and fold gently into the mixture.

Turn the mixture into the prepared pans and bake in a medium oven, 350°F, for about 45 minutes or until the cakes spring back when pressed lightly. Allow to cool in the pans for 2 minutes, then turn out on to a wire rack and leave to cool.

When cold, sandwich the cakes together with the chocolate and hazelnut spread. Dust the top with confectioners sugar.

Wholewheat Chocolate Cake

3/4 cup butter

3/4 cup light soft brown sugar

2 tablespoons molasses

3 eggs, beaten

1 cup wholewheat flour

1/3 cup cocoa powder

2 teaspoons baking soda

2 tablespoons milk

FROSTING AND DECORATION

1/2 cup butter

2/3 cup soft brown sugar

5 tablespoons water

1/4 cup cocoa powder

6 walnut halves

Grease and line an 8 inch baking pan. Cream together the butter, sugar and molasses until pale in color. Beat in the eggs, a little at a time, adding 1 tablespoon of the flour with the last amount of egg. Sift in the cocoa powder and baking soda, and fold in gently. Fold in the remaining flour and finally fold in the milk.

Turn the mixture into the prepared pan and bake in a medium oven, 350°F, for 1 hour or until the top springs back when pressed. Remove from the oven, turn out on to a wire rack and leave to cool. When cold, split the cake into two rounds.

To make the frosting, put all the ingredients, apart from the walnuts, into a pan and stir over low heat until the sugar has dissolved. Boil rapidly for 2 minutes. Remove from the heat, and allow to cool slightly, stirring frequently. Spread 2 tablespoons of the frosting over the bottom round of cake. Sandwich the two cake rounds together. When the frosting is the consistency of light cream, pour the remainder over the cake to coat the top and sides. Decorate with the walnut halves and leave to set.

Chocolate and Orange Cake

2 cups self-rising flour

¾ cup cocoa powder

1 cup unsalted butter

1¼ cups caster sugar

2 eggs, beaten

1 cup buttermilk

FILLING AND FROSTING

1 cup unsalted butter

grated rind of 1 orange

2 cups confectioners sugar, sifted

juice of ½ orange

DECORATION

fresh orange sections

Grease and line two 8–9 inch layer-cake pans. Sift together the flour and cocoa. Cream the butter and sugar until light and fluffy, then gradually beat in the eggs. Stir in the buttermilk. Fold in the flour and cocoa.

Turn the mixture into the prepared pans and bake in a medium oven, 350°F, for about 40 minutes. Remove from the oven and allow to cool in the pans for 5 minutes. Turn out on to a wire rack and leave to cool. When cold, split each cake into two layers.

To make the frosting, cream the butter with the orange rind until soft. Gradually beat in the confectioners sugar, alternately with the orange juice. Use some of the buttercream to sandwich the cakes together. Spread the remaining buttercream over the top and sides of the cake, and mark with a fork. Decorate the top of the cake with the orange sections.

Loganberry Cake

4 eggs, separated

½ cup caster sugar

¼ cup cocoa powder

1 cup fresh white breadcrumbs

1 cup ground almonds

FILLING AND TOPPING

½ cup heavy cream

4 tablespoons loganberry jam **or** conserve

DECORATION (optional)

a few fresh loganberries **or** raspberries

Grease and line an 8 inch cake pan. Beat the egg yolks and sugar until thick and creamy. Sift in the cocoa powder and fold in with the breadcrumbs. Beat the egg whites until stiff, then fold half into the mixture. Fold in the almonds, then the remainder of the egg whites, taking care to lose as little air as possible.

Turn the mixture into the prepared pan and bake in a medium oven, 350°F, for 45 minutes. Remove from the oven and allow to cool.

When the cake is quite cold, carefully split in half. Whip the cream until stiff, and fill the center of the cake with half the cream and the loganberry jam or conserve. Pipe the remaining cream over the top and decorate with fresh loganberries or raspberries, if liked.

Rum Cake

This moist chocolate cake should be served with lashings of whipped cream or Crème Chantilly (see page 108). It is best if kept for at least 24 hours before serving so that it becomes very soft and moist. Once cut, it should be eaten as soon as possible.

½ cup self-rising flour
½ teaspoon baking soda
6 tablespoons cocoa powder
3 tablespoons dark rum
6 tablespoons cold water
½ cup butter
1 cup caster sugar
2 eggs, beaten
½ cup ground almonds

Grease and line a 7½–8 inch round cake pan. Sift together the flour and baking soda. Sift the cocoa into a bowl and stir in the rum and water. Cream the butter and sugar until light and fluffy. Gradually beat in the eggs, a little at a time. Fold in the ground almonds gently, then the flour and cocoa mixture alternately.

Turn the mixture into the prepared pan and bake in a warm oven, 325°F, for about 1 hour or until the cake springs back when pressed lightly. Allow to cool in the pan for 5 minutes, then turn out on to a wire rack and leave to cool. Wrap in wax paper and foil, or store in an airtight tin until required.

Tipsy Cake

When short of time I have made this with a bought chocolate sponge cake and, whilst obviously not quite as good as a home-made sponge, it passes very well.

³/₄ cup self-rising flour

¹/₄ cup cocoa powder

4 eggs

¹/₂ cup caster sugar

3 tablespoons corn oil

SYRUP

³/₄ cup granulated sugar

2 tablespoons instant coffee granules

1¹/₂ cups water

3 tablespoons brandy **or** dark rum

1 cup whipping cream

DECORATION

coffee beans

Grease and line an 8 inch cake pan. Sift together the flour and cocoa powder. Beat the eggs and sugar until thick and creamy, and the beater leaves a trail when lifted out of the mixture. Fold in the flour and cocoa, then fold in the corn oil very carefully.

Turn the mixture into the prepared pan and bake in a medium oven, 350°F, for 45 minutes. Remove from the oven and allow to cool in the pan for 5 minutes, then turn out on to a wire rack and leave to cool.

To make the syrup, put the sugar and coffee in the water in a small pan and stir over low heat until the sugar has dissolved. Bring to the boil. Remove from the heat and add the brandy or the rum.

Place the cake on a serving plate and prick all over with a skewer. Pour over a little of the hot coffee syrup and allow it to soak in. Pour over a little more and continue doing this until all the syrup has been absorbed. Leave to stand for at least 2 hours.

Whip the cream until thick but not stiff and spread it all over the top and sides of the cake. Swirl into a pattern with a fork. Decorate with a few coffee beans.

Chocolate and Chestnut Log

This rather unusual method of making a whisked sponge produces a beautifully light cake.

¼ cup flour
¼ cup cornstarch
1½ tablespoons cocoa powder
1 teaspoon baking soda
3 eggs
1 egg white
¾ cup caster sugar

FILLING AND TOPPING

15 ounces canned unsweetened chestnut purée
¼ cup soft brown sugar
2 tablespoons dark rum
2 ounces semisweet chocolate
½ cup heavy cream
3 tablespoons light cream

Grease and line a 13 × 9 inch jelly roll pan. Sift together the flour, cornstarch, cocoa and baking powder. Beat the eggs together with the extra egg white, in a large mixing bowl. Beat in the sugar, 1 tablespoon at a time. Continue to beat until the mixture is the consistency of very lightly whipped cream. Beat in the sifted ingredients, 1 tablespoon at a time; beat well after each addition.

Turn the mixture into the prepared pan, and spread evenly. Bake in a moderately hot oven, 400°F, for about 12 minutes or until the cake springs back when pressed lightly. Turn out on to a piece of wax or non-stick silicon paper, dredged with confectioners or caster sugar. Carefully peel off the lining paper, trim off the edges, and roll up the jelly roll, keeping the paper inside the roll. Put to one side and allow to cool.

To make the filling, beat the chestnut purée with the brown sugar and rum to give a soft spreading consistency. Grate the chocolate coarsely or form into curls with a vegetable peeler (page 12). Whip the heavy and light creams together.

Unroll the jelly roll, and spread with 3 tablespoons of the cream, then the chestnut purée mixture. Sprinkle with half the grated chocolate or chocolate curls, reserving the best ones for decoration. Re-roll the jelly roll and place on a serving plate. Spread the remaining cream over the top and sides of the cake, and decorate with the remaining grated chocolate or chocolate curls.

Caribbean Gâteau

4 eggs, separated

¾ cup caster sugar

4 tablespoons very hot water (see **Note**)

¾ cup flour

¼ cup cocoa powder

1½ teaspoons baking soda

FILLING AND DECORATION

15 ounces canned mangoes

1 cup whipping cream

2 chocolate flake bars, crumbled

Grease and line an 8 inch round baking pan. Beat the egg yolks with the sugar until thick and creamy. Gradually beat in the very hot water. Beat until thick and creamy, and the beater leaves a trail when lifted out of the mixture. Sift in the flour, cocoa and baking soda, and fold in. Beat the egg whites until stiff, then fold gently into the mixture.

Turn the mixture into the prepared pan and bake in a medium oven, 350°F, for about 50 minutes, or until the cake springs back when pressed lightly. Allow to cool in the pan for 5 minutes, then turn out on to a wire rack and leave to cool. When cold, split the cake into three rounds.

To make the filling, drain the mangoes, reserving the syrup. Set aside about three of the best mango slices for decoration and chop the remainder. Whip the cream lightly with 2 tablespoons of the mango syrup.

Spread the bottom round of the cake with a third of the cream, half the chopped mango pieces and a third of the chocolate flake. Place the next layer of cake on top, and spread with another third of the cream, the mangoes and chocolate flake. Top with the last round of cake, and spread with the last of the cream. Decorate with the reserved mango slices and the remainder of the chocolate flake.

Note *It is particularly important that the water is not actually boiling. A kettle with boiling water left for a few minutes, once boiled, will be the right temperature.*

Pear and Chocolate Gâteau

3/4 cup self-rising flour

1/4 cup cocoa powder

4 eggs

1/2 cup caster sugar

FILLING AND TOPPING

4 ounces semisweet chocolate,
broken into pieces

2 egg yolks

1/2 cup whipping cream

2 ripe pears

1 tablespoon lemon juice

Make the filling first. Melt the chocolate (page 10). Remove from the heat and beat in the egg yolks, one at a time. Beat in 1 tablespoon of the cream. Whip the remainder of the cream, then fold into the chocolate mixture. Chill for 1 hour.

Grease and line two 8½–9 inch layer-cake pans. Sift together the flour and cocoa. Beat the eggs and sugar until thick and creamy and the beater leaves a trail when lifted out of the mixture. Fold in the flour.

Turn the mixture into the prepared pans. Bake in a moderately hot oven, 375°F, for 15–20 minutes, or until well risen and the cakes spring back when pressed lightly. Allow to cool in the pans for 5 minutes, then turn out on to a wire rack and leave to cool.

Peel the pears and slice them thinly. Dip in the lemon juice to preserve the color. When the cakes are quite cold, spread one of them with half the chocolate filling. Cover with two-thirds of the pears, and place the second cake on top. Spread with the last of the chocolate mixture and arrange the remaining pears on top.

Caribbean Gâteau (page 33)
OVERLEAF LEFT   Loganberry Cake (page 29)
OVERLEAF RIGHT   Peppermint Caterpillar (page 43)

Honey Cake

This cake can either be eaten warm as a dessert or cold as a cake; it is particularly good for picnics and lunchboxes.

1 cup honey
1 cup caster sugar
¼ cup butter
½ cup ale
1 egg, beaten
3 cups flour
2 teaspoons baking soda
3 teaspoons ground allspice
1 cup ground almonds

FROSTING AND DECORATION

2 ounces semisweet chocolate, broken into pieces
2 tablespoons hot water
2 tablespoons butter
1 cup confectioners sugar
1½ tablespoons cocoa powder
4 tablespoons apricot jam, sieved
½ cup blanched flaked almonds

Grease and line a 13 × 9 inch jelly roll pan. Put the honey, sugar, butter and ale in a large pan. Stir over low heat until the butter has melted and the sugar dissolved. Remove from the heat and allow to cool. Beat the egg into the mixture. Sift together the flour, baking soda and allspice, then beat gradually into the melted ingredients. Stir in the almonds.

Turn the mixture into the prepared pan and spread evenly. Bake in a moderately hot oven, 375°F, for about 20 minutes or until firm. Remove from the oven, turn out of the pan on to a wire rack (the cake should be frosted while it is still warm).

To make the frosting, melt the chocolate with the water and butter (page 10), then remove from the heat. Sift in the confectioners sugar and cocoa and beat well. Replace the bowl over the hot water to keep the frosting warm. Warm the apricot jam in a small pan. Spread evenly over the top of the cake, then spread with the frosting. Arrange the flaked almonds on the top of the cake, then cut into squares. Serve warm, or leave to cool, and store in an airtight tin.

Large and Small Cakes and Cookies
Spice Cake (page 40), Chocolate and Orange Cake (page 29), Chocolate Ginger Squares (page 46), Florentines (page 99), Shortcake Zig-zags (page 52), Chocolate Meringues (page 47) **and** *Apple Cake (page 40)*

Apple Cake

3 tart apples
juice of 1/2 lemon
2 eggs
3/4 cup caster sugar
1/2 cup butter
1/2 cup milk
6 ounces compound chocolate,
broken into pieces
1 3/4 cups flour
3 teaspoons baking soda

Grease and flour an 8 × 12 inch roasting pan. Peel, core and slice the apples thinly. Put in a bowl of cold water with the lemon juice and put to one side. Beat the eggs with 2/3 cup of the sugar until thick and creamy, and the beater leaves a trail when lifted out of the mixture.

Put the butter, milk and chocolate into a pan. Heat gently until the butter and chocolate have melted, then bring to the boil. While still boiling, pour the mixture over the eggs and sugar and stir until well blended. Sift in the flour and baking soda, and fold in carefully.

Turn the mixture into the prepared pan. Drain and dry the apple slices, and arrange them evenly over the top of the mixture (this is important – too much apple in the center and the edges will burn before the center has cooked). Sprinkle with the remaining sugar and bake in a moderately hot oven, 400°F, for about 30 minutes. Serve warm with cream, or cool in the pan, and serve sliced.

Fudgy Date Cake

3/4 cup butter
1/2 cup soft brown sugar
2 tablespoons corn syrup
3 eggs, beaten
1 3/4 cups self-rising flour, sifted
1/3 cup dried dates, chopped
4 ounces semisweet chocolate, grated
coarsely **or** chopped finely

Grease and line a 9 inch deep layer-cake pan. Cream together the butter, sugar and syrup until light and fluffy. Beat in the eggs gradually, adding 1 tablespoon of the flour with the last amount of egg. Fold in the remainder of the flour, then fold in the dates and chocolate.

Turn the mixture into the prepared pan and bake in a medium oven, 350°F, for about 45 minutes. Turn out on to a wire rack and leave to cool.

Banana and Walnut Cake

3/4 cup butter

1/2 cup caster sugar

3 eggs, beaten

1 1/2 cups self-rising flour

1/2 cup instant chocolate milk mix

1/2 cup walnuts, chopped finely

FILLING AND DECORATION

1/2 cup heavy cream

2 tablespoons milk

2 bananas

1 tablespoon lemon juice

1/4 cup confectioners sugar, sifted

extra confectioners sugar

Grease and line two 7 inch layer-cake pans. Cream the butter and sugar together until light and fluffy. Gradually beat in the eggs, a little at a time, adding 1 tablespoon of the flour with the last amount of egg. Sift in the remaining flour and the instant chocolate milk mix, and fold into the mixture. Fold in the walnuts.

Turn the mixture into the prepared pans and bake in a moderately hot oven, 375°F, for about 25 minutes. Remove from the oven and allow to cool in the pans for a couple of minutes, then turn out on to a wire rack and leave to cool.

To make the filling, whip the cream with the milk until it is just stiff. Slice the bananas and toss in the lemon juice. Fold into the cream with the confectioners sugar. Sandwich the cakes together with the banana cream and dust the top with confectioners sugar before serving.

Spice Cake

The mashed potato in this cake helps to keep it very moist.

3/4 cup butter

1 1/2 cups caster sugar

4 eggs, separated

2 ounces semisweet chocolate, broken into pieces

1 cup mashed potato

1 1/4 cups flour

1/2 teaspoon baking soda

2 teaspoons baking powder

1/2 teaspoon salt

1 teaspoon ground cinnamon

1/2 teaspoon ground nutmeg

1/2 teaspoon ground cloves

1/2 cup milk

Grease and flour a 3 pound loaf pan. Cream the butter and sugar until light and fluffy, then beat in the egg yolks. Melt the chocolate (page 10). If the potatoes are cold, heat in a non-stick skillet until lukewarm (any hotter and they will melt the butter). Beat the chocolate into the butter and sugar, then beat in the potatoes. Sift the flour with the baking powder, baking soda, salt and spices. Fold into the mixture alternately with the milk. Beat the egg whites until stiff, then fold gently into the mixture.

Turn the mixture into the prepared pan and bake in a medium oven, 350°F, for about 1 1/4 hours or until a skewer inserted into the center comes out clean. Allow to cool in the pan for 5 minutes, then turn out on to a wire rack and leave to cool. Serve sliced.

Butterfly Cake

This is the perfect recipe for anyone daunted by the thought of making novelty cakes. Although the instructions may seem complicated, it is, in fact, a very easy cake to make.

1¾ cups self-rising flour
2 teaspoons baking soda
¼ cup cocoa powder
1 cup soft margarine
1 cup caster sugar
grated rind of 1 large orange
4 eggs, beaten

BUTTERCREAM

¾ cup butter
2½ cups confectioners sugar, sifted
2 tablespoons orange juice

GLACÉ ICING

4 cups confectioners sugar
¾ cup instant chocolate milk mix
cold water

TO ASSEMBLE

2 chocolate flake bars
12 inch square cake board
2 liquorice 'pipes'

Grease and line a 9 inch square cake pan. Sift together the flour, baking soda and cocoa into a mixing bowl. Add all the remaining ingredients, and beat well for about 2 minutes.

Turn the mixture into the prepared pan and bake in a warm oven, 325°F, for about 1 hour 5 minutes, or until well risen and golden-brown. Allow to cool in the pan for 5 minutes, then turn out on to a wire rack and leave to cool.

To make the buttercream, cream the butter and beat in half the confectioners sugar. Gradually beat in the remainder of the confectioners sugar and the orange juice alternately. Split the cake into three layers. Spread the buttercream on each layer and sandwich together. To shape the butterfly's 'wings', lay the cake on a board and cut in half diagonally, then trim off about 1 inch from the corner opposite each diagonal cut. Place the two 'wings' on a wire rack with a tray underneath.

To make the glacé icing, sift 2 cups confectioners sugar with the instant chocolate milk mix into a bowl. Gradually beat in enough cold water (about 7 table-spoons) to give a thick, smooth, coating consistency. Sift the remaining confectioners sugar into a separate bowl and stir in just enough cold water to give a thick frosting for piping. Put into a small wax paper or nylon pastry bag fitted with a writing tip.

Pour the glacé icing over the two 'wings' and spread it evenly to coat the top and sides. While this frosting is still wet, pipe lines about ¾ inch apart, parallel to the straight sides of the cake on the top. Quickly draw a skewer or the point of a knife through the frosting at right angles to the piping, first in one direction and then in the other, about ¾ inch apart, wiping the knife or skewer between each line.

Trim about 1 inch off the chocolate flakes, then sandwich them together with a little glacé icing (use any that has run off the cake on to the tray underneath). Spread a narrow strip of frosting down the center of the cake board, the length of the flakes, and place them, one on top of the other, on top to form the body. While they are still wet, carefully lift the 'wings' off the rack using two spatulas, and place them in position on the board. Cover the ends of the liquorice pipes with a little frosting and place in position for the antennae. Leave to set for at least 2 hours.

Peppermint Caterpillar

3 eggs

1/3 cup caster sugar

2/3 cup self-rising flour

2 tablespoons cocoa powder

FILLING AND DECORATION

1½ cups butter

5 cups confectioners sugar, sifted

peppermint extract

a little green coloring

1 ounce semisweet chocolate,
broken into small pieces

Grease and line a 13 × 9 inch jelly roll pan. Place a paper cake case, about 2–3 inches wide, on a cookie sheet. Beat the eggs and sugar until thick and creamy, and the beater leaves a trail when lifted out of the mixture. Sift in the flour and cocoa, and fold in.

Put 1 heaping tablespoon of the mixture into the paper cake case and turn the remainder of the cake mixture into the prepared pan. Spread evenly. Bake both cakes in a moderately hot oven, 400°F, for about 10 minutes or until the cake springs back when pressed lightly. Remove both the jelly roll and the small individual cake from the oven. Turn the jelly roll on to a piece of wax or non-stick silicon paper, dredged with confectioners or caster sugar. Carefully peel off the lining paper, trim off the edges and quickly roll up the jelly roll lengthways, (ie to make a long thin, rather than a short fat, roll), keeping the paper inside the roll. Allow to cool, Cool the small cake.

To make the filling, cream the butter, beat in the confectioners sugar, then beat in the peppermint extract and coloring. Unroll the jelly roll, spread with one-third of the filling and re-roll. Taper one end of the roll to make the caterpillar's tail by shaving off a little of the cake from either side. Peel off the case of the small cake and spread its base with a little of the remaining filling. Place on the fatter end of the roll to make the caterpillar's head. Spread all but 3 tablespoons of the frosting over the cakes.

Melt the chocolate (page 10) and cool slightly. Beat into the remaining frosting, then put into a wax paper or nylon pastry bag fitted with a writing tip. Pipe lines across the jelly roll to make segments for the caterpillar's body, and pipe in eyes and a mouth. Leave to set.

Refrigerator Cookie Cake

I was given this recipe in the late 1960s by the late James Robertson Justice's mother who had served it to members of the Royal Family when they had lunched with her in Scotland.

4 ounces semisweet chocolate,
broken into small pieces.

¾ cup unsalted butter

3 egg yolks

⅓ cup caster sugar

6 tablespoons water

1 tablespoon granulated sugar

½ cup warm strong black coffee

2 tablespoons dark rum

32 Oreo cookies

DECORATION
chocolate vermicelli

Melt the chocolate (page 10). Remove from the heat and allow to cool slightly. Cream the butter until light and fluffy, then beat in the chocolate.

In a separate bowl, beat the egg yolks lightly. Put the caster sugar and water into a small, heavy-based pan and stir over low heat until the sugar has dissolved. Boil rapidly to 225°F on a candy thermometer (thread stage). Beat into the egg yolks gradually until the mixture has a mousse-like consistency. Add to the butter mixture, a little at a time, and beat well.

Dissolve the granulated sugar in the coffee and add the rum. Quickly dip eight cookies into the coffee syrup and place flat on a plate in two rows. Spread with a little of the chocolate buttercream. Repeat these layers twice more, then finish with a layer of cookies. Spread the remaining chocolate buttercream over the top and sides, and sprinkle with chocolate vermicelli.

Chill in a refrigerator for 2 hours or until quite firm.

Small Cakes and Cookies

Although one can buy any number of excellent cookies, there is nothing quite like home-made cookies in the tin. In fact, I try not to make them too often as they are so more-ish and the temptation to have one with a cup of tea or coffee becomes too great. However, if you are strong-willed or do not have to watch your weight, they are a great standby, as most of them keep well in an airtight tin, or can be frozen and do not take long to defrost.

As well as making the recipes I have given here, you may like to try coating one side of any of your favorite shop cookies with chocolate. This is a good way for young children to do some 'cooking' without using the oven and generally making havoc. Melt some compound chocolate for them and let them spread it on shop cookies; they will keep quietly busy for ages, even if they do get a bit sticky!

As I prefer moist, rich chocolate cakes I have not included many small cakes; these have a tendency to dryness and can be very fiddly to frost and decorate. An exception is Cherry Fingers (page 48), which count among my favorite cakes. They have the essential qualities of moistness and richness, are made with instant chocolate milk mix and ground almonds, and have an unusual filling of cream cheese and cherry jam.

A useful idea for a quick, delicious and sustaining snack is to put one or two pieces of chocolate – preferably bittersweet chocolate – into a chunk of very fresh French bread. This is perfect for picnics, long journeys and other occasions when you need something to keep you going but do not have the facilities for elaborate preparations. I first had a 'chocolate sandwich' like this when I was a child in France on an exchange visit. Most of the adults had gone to visit an elderly relative and we had been left to amuse ourselves in the village. This is what we had for supper, and I have never forgotten it.

Chocolate Ginger Squares

1¼ cups flour

¼ cup cocoa powder

½ teaspoon salt

2 teaspoons baking soda

½ cup light soft brown sugar

2 eggs, separated

6 tablespoons corn oil

6 tablespoons milk

2 tablespoons candied ginger, chopped finely

FROSTING

2 tablespoons butter

¼ cup cocoa powder

3 tablespoons hot water

2 cups confectioners sugar, sifted

2 tablespoons candied ginger, chopped finely

Grease and line a 7 inch square cake pan. Sift together the flour, cocoa, salt and baking soda into a bowl. Add the sugar. Blend the egg yolks, oil and milk. Pour into the center of the dry ingredients and beat well. Mix in the ginger. Beat the egg whites until stiff, then fold gently into the mixture.

Turn the mixture into the prepared pan and bake in a medium oven, 350°F, for about 45 minutes, or until well risen and firm. Remove from the oven, allow to cool in the pan for 5 minutes, then turn out on to a wire rack and leave to cool.

To make the frosting, melt the butter in a pan. Blend the cocoa with the hot, not boiling, water, then pour into the confectioners sugar. Add the butter and beat well to give a thick glossy frosting (use a little extra water if necessary). Add the ginger and beat well. Pour evenly over the top of the cake. Leave to set. Cut into squares to serve.

Makes 9

Crunchy Date Bars

½ pound graham crackers

½ cup butter

3 tablespoons Demerara sugar

2 cups dried dates, chopped

¼ cup raisins

4 ounces semisweet chocolate **or** compound chocolate, broken into pieces

Lightly butter a 9 inch layer-cake pan. Put the graham crackers in a polythene bag and crush with a rolling-pin, or use a food processor. Heat the butter and sugar gently in a pan until the butter has melted and the sugar dissolved. Remove from the heat and add the dates and raisins. Stir in the cracker crumbs and blend well.

Spread the mixture evenly over the base of the prepared pan and press down firmly. Melt the chocolate (page 10) and spread over the cookie mixture. Mark out bars with a sharp knife while the chocolate is still slightly soft. Leave to set for at least 1 hour. Cut into bars to serve.

Makes 10

Chocolate Meringues

These meringues look very attractive on a serving plate mixed with plain meringues. Alternatively, sandwich one plain and one chocolate meringue together.

3 egg whites
1/3 cup caster sugar
3/4 cup sugar
1/4 cup cocoa powder
1/4 cup whipping cream (optional)

Lightly oil a cookie sheet and line with non-stick silicon paper. Beat the egg whites until they form stiff peaks. Gradually beat in the caster sugar, 1 teaspoon at a time until the mixture is stiff and shiny. Sift together the confectioners sugar and cocoa and fold into the mixture.

Either put the mixture in a pastry bag fitted with a large rose tip, and pipe 12 meringues on to the prepared cookie sheet, or put 12 heaping spoonfuls of the mixture on to the cookie sheet. Bake in a very cool oven, 250°F, for 1 hour. Reduce the heat as much as possible and cook for a further 4 hours, or until the meringues are quite dry. Remove from the oven and allow to cool. For serving, whip the cream lightly, if used, and sandwich the meringues together, two at a time, with the cream.

Makes 6

Coconut Meringue Slices

1/2 cup butter **or** margarine
2 cups flour, sifted
cold water
1 3/4 cups semisweet chocolate chips
2 egg whites
1/2 cup caster sugar
1 cup shredded coconut

Rub the fat into the flour until the mixture resembles fine breadcrumbs. Bind with cold water to form a firm dough. Roll out on a floured surface and use to line the base and sides of a 7 × 11 inch jelly roll pan. Sprinkle the chocolate over the pastry. Beat the egg whites until they form stiff peaks, then beat in half the sugar, 1 teaspoon at a time until the mixture is stiff and shiny. Fold in the remaining sugar and the coconut. Spoon it over the chocolate and spread evenly, using a spatula, until the chocolate is completely covered.

Bake in a medium oven, 350°F, for 30 minutes. Remove from the oven and allow to cool slightly. Cut into slices while still warm.

Makes 14

Cherry Fingers

A good quality cherry jam makes all the difference to these fingers.

³/₄ cup butter

³/₄ cup caster sugar

4 eggs, separated

a pinch of salt

1 cup instant chocolate milk mix

¹/₂ cup ground almonds

¹/₄ cup flour, sifted

FILLING AND DECORATION

¹/₄ cup butter

¹/₄ cup cream cheese

¹/₂ cup confectioners sugar, sifted

4 tablespoons good quality bing cherry jam

extra confectioners sugar

Grease and line a 13 × 9 inch jelly roll pan. Cream the butter and sugar until light and fluffy. Beat in the egg yolks with the salt, one at a time. Sift in the instant chocolate milk mix, and fold in. Fold in the ground almonds and flour. Beat the egg whites until stiff, then fold in gently, a third at a time (the mixture may look curdled at this stage, but this does not matter).

Turn the mixture into the prepared pan and spread evenly. Bake in a medium oven, 350°F, for about 25 minutes. Turn out on to a sheet of wax paper on a wire tray. Peel off the lining paper carefully. Leave to cool, then cut the cake in half to make two squares.

To make the filling, cream the butter with the cream cheese and confectioners sugar. Spread over one of the squares of cake. Spread the cherry jam on top and sandwich the cakes together. Cut in half, then cut each half into eight fingers. Dust with confectioners sugar before serving.

Makes 16

Chocolate and Almond Slices

1¾ cups flour

1 teaspoon baking soda

¼ cup cocoa powder

½ cup butter

½ cup soft brown sugar

2 tablespoons corn syrup

a little milk

¼ cup flaked almonds

Well butter an 11 × 7 inch jelly roll pan. Sift together the flour, baking soda and cocoa. Cream the butter and sugar until light and fluffy, then beat in the syrup. Gradually work in the dry ingredients to make a smooth dough.

Press into the prepared pan and prick all over with a fork. Brush with a little milk and sprinkle with the almonds. Bake in a medium oven, 350°F, for about 30 minutes or until golden-brown, then cool in the tin and mark into fingers while still warm.

Makes 18

Mixed Nut Slice

⅓ cup butter

2 tablespoons caster sugar

1 egg yolk

½ teaspoon vanilla extract

1 cup flour

1 tablespoon cocoa powder

FILLING

2 eggs

½ cup soft brown sugar

¾ cup chopped mixed nuts

¾ cup shredded coconut

TOPPING

2 tablespoons chopped mixed nuts

2 tablespoons shredded coconut

¾ cup semisweet **or** milk chocolate bits, broken into pieces

Butter a 7 × 11 inch jelly roll pan. Cream the butter and sugar until light and fluffy, then beat in the egg yolk and vanilla extract. Sift in the flour and cocoa and form into a stiff dough. Turn on to a lightly floured surface and knead lightly. Roll out to a rectangle a little smaller than the pan, then lift into the pan and press into the edges.

To make the filling, beat the eggs and sugar until thick and creamy, and the beater leaves a trail when lifted out of the mixture. Fold in the nuts and coconut, then spread evenly over the chocolate base. Sprinkle with the nuts and coconut for the topping.

Bake in a moderately hot oven, 375°F for 20–25 minutes or until golden-brown. Remove from the oven and allow to cool in the pan. When cold, cut into 15 squares.

Melt the chocolate bits and drizzle over the nut bars (page 13). Leave to set.

Makes 15

Chocolate Croissants

1 teaspoon sugar
*¹/₃ cup **plus** 1 tablespoon warm water*
2 teaspoons dried yeast
2 cups bread flour
1 teaspoon salt
2 tablespoons shortening
¹/₄ cup caster sugar
1 egg, lightly beaten
¹/₃ cup butter
¹/₂ cup milk chocolate bits
1 egg

EGG GLAZE

1 tablespoon water
¹/₂ teaspoon caster sugar

Dissolve the sugar in the water in a bowl, sprinkle with the yeast and leave in a warm place for 10 minutes or until frothy. Sift together the flour and salt, rub in the shortening and mix in the sugar. Make a well in the center of the flour, pour in the yeast liquid and the egg, and mix to a soft dough. Turn on to a lightly floured surface and knead well for about 5 minutes. When the dough feels smooth and elastic, roll it out to a rectangle about 12 × 5 inches.

Divide the butter into three. Dot the top two-thirds of the dough with one part of the butter, cut into small pieces. Fold the bottom third up and the top third down, like an envelope. Seal the edges, give the dough a half turn, then roll out again and repeat this process with the remaining two parts of butter. Fold the dough, put into an oiled polythene bag and chill for at least 1 hour.

Roll out to a 12 inch square, cover with a piece of oiled clingfilm and leave for 10–15 minutes. Trim the edges, divide into four squares, then divide each of these into two triangles.

To make the egg glaze, beat the egg with the water and sugar. Brush all over the dough, then sprinkle with the chocolate bits. Roll each triangle up loosely, starting from the wide side and going towards the point.

Place the croissants on oiled cookie sheets, with the tip underneath, and curve into crescents. Brush again with the egg glaze and cover with oiled clingfilm. Put in a warm place and leave until the dough has doubled in size, then remove the clingfilm, brush again with the egg glaze and bake in a hot oven, 425°F for 15–20 minutes or until well risen and golden-brown. Remove from the oven and cool on a wire rack.

Makes 8

Chocolate Chip Cookies

I really like the texture of these cookies – the outside edges become very crisp while the center stays deliciously soft.

½ cup butter

½ cup caster sugar

1 egg, beaten

½ teaspoon vanilla extract

1 ¼ cups wholewheat flour

a pinch of salt

3 tablespoons milk

1 cup semisweet chocolate bits

Well grease three or four large cookie sheets. Cream the butter and sugar until light and fluffy. Beat in the egg and vanilla extract gradually. Sift in the flour and salt, and fold in with the milk and chocolate bits.

Put spoonfuls of the mixture on to the prepared cookie sheets, spacing them well apart. Bake in a medium oven, 350°F, for about 12–15 minutes or until golden-brown. Leave to cool on the cookie sheets for 1 minute, then remove with a spatula and cool on a wire rack.

Makes about 36

Chocolate Chip Shortcake

1 cup flour

½ cup cornstarch

¼ cup caster sugar

½ cup butter

¼ cup milk chocolate bits

Sift together the flour and cornstarch. Add the sugar, then rub in the butter. The mixture will become crumbly at first, but continue working it until it clings together in heavy lumps. Turn on to a board or working surface dusted with flour or cornstarch and knead lightly. Place the ball on a buttered cookie sheet and roll out to make a 9 inch circle. Prick the surface with a fork. Mark out 10 portions with a sharp knife and flute the edges with your fingers. Sprinkle with the chocolate bits.

Bake in a warm oven, 325°F, for 30–35 minutes or until the shortcake is cooked; but it should not be browned. Remove from the oven and leave to cool on the cookie sheet for 10 minutes, then, using a spatula, lift carefully on to a wire rack to cool.

Makes 10

Pineapple Shortcakes

1¼ cups flour
¾ cup instant cocoa powder
a pinch of salt
½ cup butter
½ cup heavy cream
2 cups canned pineapple rings, drained

Sift together the flour, instant cocoa powder and salt. Rub in the butter until the mixture is crumbly, then knead together until smooth. Roll out on a floured surface and cut into eight 4 inch diameter circles.

Put the shortcakes on to greased cookie sheets and bake in a warm oven, 325°F, for about 15 minutes. Remove from the oven and allow to cool on the sheet for 5 minutes. Transfer to a wire rack and leave to cool. Whip the cream until stiff, and divide between the cookies. Cut the pineapple rings into quarters and place two pieces on each cookie.

Makes 8

Shortcake Zig-Zags

1¼ cups flour
¼ cup caster sugar
½ cup butter
2 tablespoons instant cocoa powder

Well butter a 7 inch square cake pan. Sift all but 2 tablespoons of the flour into a bowl. Add the sugar, then rub in the butter until the mixture is crumbly. Divide the mixture in half. Work in the remaining flour to one half and the instant cocoa powder to the other. Turn on to a board or working surface lightly dusted with flour, and knead each dough separately until smooth. Roll out and cut into strips 1½ inches wide. Put these strips diagonally across the pan; any trimming can be cut into shapes and baked on a cookie sheet.

Bake in a warm oven, 325°F, for about 30–35 minutes, or until crisp but not brown (trimmings will only take about 5 minutes). Remove from the oven, mark out into bars and leave to cool in the pan.

Makes 12

Chocolate Cookie Squares

A very popular recipe of my mother's, who makes these endlessly.

6 ounces Oreo cookies
1/2 cup butter
1/3 cup corn syrup
1/4 cup cocoa powder
1/2 cup seedless raisins
1/2 cup candied cherries, chopped finely
1/4 cup blanched almonds, chopped
25 chocolate chips

Grease a shallow 7 inch square cake pan. Put the cookies in a polythene bag and crush with a rolling-pin, or use a food processor. Heat the butter, syrup and cocoa, gently until the fat has melted. Remove from the heat and stir in first the raisins, cherries and almonds and then the cookie crumbs. Stir until thoroughly mixed.

Press the mixture into the prepared pan and space the chocolate chips evenly on top in lines of five. Leave in a cool place to set, then cut into squares, between the chips.

Makes 25

Chocolate Sandwich Cookies

1/2 cup butter
1/2 cup caster sugar
2 tablespoons beaten egg
1/2 teaspoon vanilla extract
2 cups flour, sifted

FILLING
1/3 cup butter
3/4 cup soft brown sugar
1 cup semisweet chocolate bits

Cream together the butter and sugar until pale and creamy. Beat in the egg and vanilla extract, a little at a time, alternating with some of the flour. Stir in the remaining flour to give a firm dough. Knead the dough until smooth, then roll out on a floured surface to a thickness of about 1/4 inch. Stamp out circles with a 2 inch fluted cookie cutter.

Place the circles on greased cookie sheets and prick with a fork. Re-roll the trimmings and cut out more cookies. Bake in a medium oven, 350°F for about 15 minutes until golden. Leave on the sheets to harden for a few minutes, then remove to a wire rack and allow to cool.

To make the filling, beat together the butter and sugar until pale and creamy. Melt the chocolate (page 10). Beat into the creamed mixture, then leave to thicken slightly. Sandwich the cookies together two at a time, with some of the chocolate frosting.

Makes about 20

Hot Desserts

Hot desserts must be amongst the most nostalgic foods for all of us, recalling to memory favorite meals of childhood days. But some hot desserts, such as hot chocolate soufflé, are nothing if not sophisticated.

It can be difficult to get the timing of these dishes right, especially if you are entertaining and do not want to be in the kitchen just before serving the meal. Steamed puddings should be prepared well in advance. Soufflés too can be planned ahead, if you put them in a *cold* oven and increase the cooking time accordingly as they have a long time to cook. You can make up the soufflé up to 24 hours in advance and keep it in a refrigerator. To cook, put it in a cold oven. Set the oven to the required temperature. As it heats up, so will the soufflé, which will rise slowly. If a cold soufflé mixture is put into a hot oven, a seal is quickly formed over the top of it, preventing the soufflé from rising.

Most hot chocolate desserts are improved if served with pouring or spooning cream, lightly whipped heavy cream – sweetened if liked – ice cream or a hot chocolate sauce.

Steamed Chocolate Pudding with Orange Sauce (page 63)
OVERLEAF LEFT   Marbled Savarin (page 80)
OVERLEAF RIGHT   Tia Maria Soufflé (page 79)
***and** Avocado Fool (page 73)*

Hot Chocolate Soufflé

*4 ounces semisweet chocolate, broken
into pieces*

2 tablespoons water **or** *liqueur*

½ cup caster sugar

4 eggs, separated

confectioners sugar

Butter a 1 quart soufflé dish. Melt the chocolate with the water or liqueur (page 10). Beat together the sugar and egg yolks until thick and pale. Beat in the melted chocolate until well blended. Beat the egg whites until stiff, then fold very gently into the chocolate mixture.

Pour the mixture into the prepared soufflé dish and bake in a moderately hot oven, 375°F, for about 30 minutes until well risen and firm, but slightly wobbly. Dust the top with confectioners sugar and serve at once.

Serves 4

Note *An extra egg white will make the soufflé even lighter.*

Hot Cocoa and Orange Soufflé

2 tablespoons butter **or** *margarine*

¼ cup flour, sifted

½ cup milk

¼ cup cocoa powder

⅓ cup caster sugar

grated rind and juice of 1 orange

4 eggs, separated

confectioners sugar

Butter a 1½ quart soufflé dish. Melt the fat in a pan and stir in the flour. Add the milk and bring to the boil, stirring until thick and smooth. Add the cocoa, sugar and grated orange rind and juice. Return to the boil, stirring until well blended, then remove from the heat and leave to cool. Add the egg yolks, one at a time, beating until smooth. Beat the egg whites until stiff, then fold gently into the chocolate sauce.

Pour the mixture into the prepared soufflé dish. Bake in a moderate oven, 350°F, for about 45 minutes until well risen and firm, but slightly wobbly. Dust the top with confectioners sugar and serve at once.

Serves 4

Strawberry Chocolate Box (page 70)

Chocolate Soufflé Tart

1½ cups flour

a pinch of salt

⅓ cup butter

cold water

FILLING

2 eggs, separated

2 tablespoons caster sugar

1 tablespoon cornstarch

1 cup light cream

4 ounces semisweet chocolate,
grated coarsely

Sift together the flour and salt, and rub in the butter until the mixture resembles fine breadcrumbs. Bind together with cold water to make a firm dough. Turn on to a floured surface and knead lightly until smooth. Roll out and use to line an 8 inch flan pan. Prebake in a moderately hot oven, 375°F, for 20 minutes.

To make the filling, mix together the egg yolks, sugar and cornstarch. Beat in the cream, then stir in the chocolate, and blend well. Beat the egg whites until they form stiff peaks. Fold gently into the mixture, then turn into the baked pastry case. Bake at 375°F for 25–35 minutes or until the mixture is well risen and golden-brown. Serve with cream.

Serves 6

Baked Pears

½ cup water

¼ cup sugar

1 vanilla pod

6 large pears, peeled, cored and quartered

4 ounces semisweet chocolate,
broken into pieces

2 tablespoons butter

Butter a baking pan. Put the water, sugar and vanilla pod into a pan over low heat and stir until the sugar has dissolved. Bring to the boil. Add the pears and poach gently for 10 minutes.

Melt the chocolate with the butter (page 10). Stir in 2 tablespoons of the juice from the pan. Drain the pears, discarding the vanilla pod, and place in the prepared pan. Pour over the melted chocolate, cover and bake in a medium oven, 350°F, for 15 minutes. Serve with ice cream or cream.

Serves 4–6

Baked Hazelnut and Cherry Pudding

½ cup hazelnuts

¾ cup butter **or** margarine

¾ cup light soft brown sugar

3 eggs

1¼ cups self-rising flour

¼ cup cocoa powder

1 pound frozen pitted bing cherries, thawed and drained **or** 1 pound canned pitted bing cherries, drained but reserving 4 tablespoons syrup

Well butter a baking pan approximately 8–9 inches in diameter. Chop the hazelnuts very finely, or grind in a blender or food processor until they resemble coarse breadcrumbs. Cream the fat and the sugar until light and fluffy. Beat in the eggs, a little at a time, adding 1 tablespoon of the flour with the last amount of egg. Sift together the flour and cocoa and fold in alternately with the cherries and nuts.

Turn the mixture into the prepared pan and bake in a medium oven, 350°F, for about 45 minutes until well risen and firm to the touch. Turn out and serve with whipped cream.

Serves 6

Chocolate Eve's Pudding

This combination of blackcurrant and chocolate quite transforms this standard dessert.

12 ounces fresh **or** frozen blackcurrants, thawed

⅓ cup Demerara sugar

½ cup butter **or** margarine

½ cup caster sugar

2 eggs, beaten

¾ cup self-rising flour

¼ cup cocoa powder

Butter a baking pan approximately 7–8 inches in diameter. Put in the blackcurrants and sprinkle with the sugar. Cream the fat and the sugar until light and fluffy. Beat in the eggs, a little at a time, adding 1 tablespoon of the flour with the last amount of egg. Sift in the flour and cocoa and fold into the mixture.

Spoon the mixture over the blackcurrants and spread evenly. Bake in a medium oven, 350°F, for about 40 minutes. Serve with cream.

Serves 4–6

Saucy Sponge Pudding

Do not be alarmed by the rather strange way in which this pudding is made! During cooking, the cake mixture rises above the cocoa/water and sugar mixture to give a light sponge on top with a rich chocolate sauce underneath.

¾ cup self-rising flour
¼ cup cocoa powder
a pinch of salt
1 teaspoon baking soda
½ cup soft margarine
½ cup soft brown sugar
2 eggs
½ teaspoon vanilla extract
1 tablespoon milk

SAUCE

½ cup soft brown sugar
¼ cup cocoa powder
1 cup hot water

Well butter a 1 quart baking pan. Sift together the flour, cocoa, salt and baking soda into a mixing bowl. Add the margarine and sugar. Beat the eggs with the vanilla extract and milk, add to the remaining ingredients and beat well for 2 minutes until thoroughly mixed. Spoon into the prepared dish.

To make the sauce, blend together the sugar and cocoa, then gradually stir in the water, and mix well. Pour over the sponge mixture. Bake in a moderately hot oven, 375°F, for 30–40 minutes. Serve with cream.

Serves 4–6

Sussex Pudding

2 cups self-rising flour
½ teaspoon salt
¾ cup shredded suet
½ cup water (approx)
½ cup butter, preferably unsalted
2 tablespoons soft brown sugar
¼ cup instant cocoa powder

Well butter a 1 quart pudding bowl. Sift together the flour and salt. Add the suet, then bind with the water to make a soft, but not sticky, dough. Roll out to an 8 inch circle and use to line the prepared bowl.

Cream the butter, then beat in the sugar and instant cocoa powder. Form into a ball and put in the middle of the bowl. Dampen the edges of the pastry, then fold over and press together, so that the chocolate ball is completely enclosed. Cover with a double layer of buttered wax paper or with foil, and steam for 2½–3 hours (add more water to the pan if necessary). Turn out and serve with cream.

Serves 4–6

Steamed Chocolate Pudding with Orange Sauce

The light mousse-like orange sauce makes all the difference to this fairly basic steamed pudding.

1 medium-sized orange
¾ cup butter
¾ cup caster sugar
3 eggs, beaten
1¼ cups self-rising flour
¼ cup cocoa powder

SAUCE
2 tablespoons butter, preferably unsalted
grated rind and juice of 1 orange
2 teaspoons flour
¼ cup caster sugar
1 egg, separated

DECORATION (optional)
orange rind, pared

Well butter a 1 quart pudding bowl. Thinly pare the orange rind, then cut into matchstick pieces. Cream together the butter, sugar and orange shreds until the mixture is light and fluffy. Beat in the eggs, a little at a time, adding 1 tablespoon of flour with the last amount of egg. Sift in the remaining flour and the cocoa and fold into the mixture.

Turn the mixture into the prepared bowl, cover with a double piece of buttered wax paper or with foil, and steam for 1¾–2 hours (add more water to the pan if necessary). Turn out of the bowl and serve with the orange sauce and orange rind, if used.

To make the sauce, cream the butter with the orange rind and gradually beat in the flour mixed with the sugar, then add the egg yolk. Make the orange juice up to ½ cup with water, and beat into the mixture; it does not matter if the mixture looks curdled at this stage. Turn the mixture into a small, heavy-based pan and cook over low heat, stirring all the time, until the sauce thickens. Cover the pan with foil and put to one side until ready to serve, then re-heat gently. Beat the egg white until stiff and fold gently into the sauce just before serving.

Serves 6

VARIATION   *Add 2 tablespoons Cointreau or Grand Marnier to the sauce in place of 2 tablespoons water.*

Rich Chocolate Fondue

Chocolate fondue must be one of the greatest delights for real chocoholics, so I have deliberately chosen a really rich one here.
What you choose to dip into your fondue is entirely a matter of personal preference, and although diced squares of cake, ladyfingers etc, (which may be more suitable for children) can be used, I personally prefer fresh fruit. Cubes of pineapple, whole fresh strawberries, slices of apples, peaches and pears, orange sections etc, are all delicious dipped into the fondue.

8 ounces semisweet chocolate, broken into pieces

½ cup heavy cream

1½ tablespoons rum, brandy or liqueur, eg Tia Maria, Grand Marnier or Cointreau

3 tablespoons blanched almonds, finely chopped

FOR DIPPING

2 pounds prepared fresh fruit (see above)

Place the chocolate in a fondue pot with the cream, and heat very gently, stirring until the chocolate has melted. Stir in the rum, brandy or liqueur and the nuts, then stand over a very gentle flame on a fondue stand.

Use fondue forks to skewer the fruit to dip into the fondue, and serve with crisp cookies or wafers and whipped cream, if liked.

Serves 6

Milk Chocolate Fondue

7 ounces compound chocolate, broken into pieces

grated rind of 1 orange

½ cup light cream

FOR DIPPING

2 pounds prepared fresh or canned fruit or ladyfingers or squares of sponge cake

Place the chocolate in a fondue pot with the orange rind and cream, and heat very gently, stirring until the chocolate has melted. Remove from the heat and place over a very gentle flame on a fondue stand.

Use fondue forks to skewer the fruit, cake or cookies.

Serves 6

Cold Desserts and Ices

Many people, who would not think twice about enjoying a variety of fruit fillings in a box of candies, have surprisingly conservative ideas about teaming up chocolate with different fruits for desserts. However, there are few fruits that chocolate does not accompany successfully, unless it has such a delicate flavor that the chocolate completely overpowers it. I have, therefore, deliberately tried to include as wide a variety of fruit as possible.

For me, the finest of all cold chocolate desserts is the chocolate mousse; easy to make, quick to set and, above all, rich and delicious. Other devotees are numerous, which is why there are no less than seven mousse recipes in this chapter, plus the Pots de Chocolat on page 109.

Iced desserts are also, of course, extremely popular. Although one can buy excellent commercially produced ice cream, there is nothing to beat home-made. I make no excuses for the fact that, with few exceptions, they are all fairly extravagant, being made with eggs and fresh cream. If you are going to go to the extra trouble of making it yourself, the result must be superb.

Do look also at the Large Cakes and Gâteaux in the book as well as the classic recipes. Many of these make excellent desserts.

Crunchy Chocolate Mousse

This is a very economical chocolate mousse, not rich and, therefore, excellent for children.

1 envelope gelatin
4 tablespoons cold water
1½ cups milk
3 eggs, separated
2 tablespoons caster sugar
½ teaspoon vanilla extract
4 ounces semisweet chocolate, broken into small pieces

TOPPING

2 tablespoons butter
½ cup fresh brown breadcrumbs
2 tablespoons soft brown sugar

Sprinkle the gelatin over the water in a bowl and leave to soften for 5 minutes. Pour the milk into a pan and bring up to blood temperature. Beat the egg yolks with the sugar and vanilla extract in a bowl or the top of a double boiler until thick and creamy. Pour in the milk. Put over a pan of gently simmering water and cook until the custard has thickened, stirring all the time. Stir in the softened gelatin and, when this has dissolved, add the chocolate, and stir until melted. Remove from the heat and put to one side until the mixture begins to thicken. Stir from time to time.

Beat the egg whites until they form stiff peaks, then fold into the chocolate mixture. Turn into a shallow serving bowl and chill in a refrigerator for at least 1 hour or until set.

To make the topping, melt the butter in a skillet and fry the breadcrumbs until crisp and golden, stirring frequently. Remove from the heat and stir in the sugar. Sprinkle the crumbs over the mousse shortly before serving.

Serves 6–8

VARIATION   *Spread a layer of whipped cream between the mousse and the fried breadcrumbs.*

Chocolate and Crème de Menthe Mousses

10 ounces semisweet chocolate,
broken into pieces

4 eggs, separated

3 tablespoons crème de menthe

DECORATION
chocolate curls (page 12)

Place 12 paper cake cases in muffin pans. Melt 6 ounces of the chocolate (page 10). Divide between the paper cases and, with the back of a teaspoon, spread evenly over the base and sides of the cases. Put in a cool place for at least 30 minutes, or until the chocolate is quite hard.

Peel off the paper cases carefully. Melt the remaining chocolate (page 10) and remove from the heat. Beat in the egg yolks and the crème de menthe. Beat the egg whites until they form stiff peaks, then fold into the chocolate mixture. Spoon into the prepared cases and chill in a refrigerator for at least 1 hour. Decorate each mousse with a chocolate curl before serving.

Makes 12

Bitter Chocolate and Orange Mousse

If you enjoy fresh orange juice, this mousse looks very attractive set in halved orange shells.

6 ounces bittersweet chocolate,
broken into pieces

grated rind and juice of 1 large orange

1 tablespoon cocoa powder

2 tablespoons Grand Marnier **or** Cointreau

3 eggs, separated

1/2 cup heavy cream

DECORATION
whipped cream (optional)

grated orange rind **or** thin matchsticks of
orange rind

Melt the chocolate (page 10) with the orange rind and juice and the cocoa. Remove from the heat and beat in the liqueur and egg yolks. Whip the cream until it holds its shape, and beat the egg whites until stiff. Fold, first, the cream and then the egg whites into the chocolate mixture. Turn into six ramekins and chill in a refrigerator for at least 1 hour. Decorate each mousse with a heaping teaspoonful of whipped cream, if liked and a little orange rind before serving.

Serves 6

Almond Mousse

A chocolate mousse made very special by the burnt almonds.

*6 ounces semisweet **or** compound chocolate, broken into pieces*

½ cup butter, preferably unsalted

½ cup caster sugar

2 eggs, separated

1½ cups ground almonds

½ cup heavy cream

DECORATION

½ cup blanched whole almonds

½ cup heavy cream

Thoroughly clean and polish a 1 pint jelly mold. Melt the chocolate (page 10), and use to coat the inside of the mold, as when making Easter eggs (page 15); you may find it easier to do this in two layers. When the chocolate is hard, remove from the mold, (do not worry if it cracks very slightly as you can hide this with piping when decorating).

Cream together the butter and sugar until light and fluffy, then beat in the egg yolks, one at a time. Fold in the ground almonds. Whip the cream lightly until it holds its shape. Beat the egg whites until stiff. Fold, first, the cream and then the egg whites into the mixture. Turn into the chocolate mold and chill in a refrigerator for at least 2 hours.

Invert the mold on to a serving plate. Put the almonds on a piece of foil and toast under the broiler until *very lightly* burnt. Remove and leave to cool. Whip the cream until stiff, and pile on the top and edges of the chocolate mold. Decorate with the burnt almonds.

Serves 6–8

Chocolate and Raspberry Layer Mousse

When I make this, I often set it in a glass bowl and, while the raspberry mousse is setting, I tilt the bowl on its side so that the mousse sets diagonally across the bowl. I then pour the chocolate mousse on top and stand the bowl upright to give a diagonal effect. Alternatively, it can be set in individual glasses.

RASPBERRY MOUSSE
¾ pound fresh raspberries

1½ teaspoons powdered gelatin

2 tablespoons cold water

2 eggs, separated

¼ cup caster sugar

*½ cup heavy **or** whipping cream*

CHOCOLATE MOUSSE
6 ounces semisweet chocolate, broken into pieces

2 teaspoons instant coffee granules

1 tablespoon water

4 eggs, separated

*½ cup heavy **or** whipping cream*

DECORATION
½ cup whipped cream (optional)

a few fresh raspberries

Rub the raspberries through a sieve or purée in a blender or food processor. Sprinkle the gelatin over the cold water in a bowl and leave to soften for 5 minutes. Stand over a pan of simmering water and leave until the gelatin has dissolved. Remove from the heat and allow to cool slightly. Beat the egg yolks with the sugar until thick and creamy, then beat in the gelatin. Stir in the raspberry purée and blend well. Whip the cream lightly until it holds its shape. Beat the egg whites until stiff. Fold, first, the cream and then the egg whites into the raspberry mixture. Pour into a glass bowl, and chill in a refrigerator for about 30 minutes.

Melt the chocolate with the coffee granules and water (page 10). Remove from the heat and beat in the egg yolks. Whip the cream lightly until it forms soft peaks. Beat the egg whites until stiff. Fold, first, the cream and then the egg whites into the chocolate mixture. Pour over the raspberry mousse, and chill for at least 1 hour. Decorate with whipped cream, if liked, and raspberries before serving.

Serves 6–8

Strawberry Chocolate Box

With imported strawberries available throughout the year, this is a superb and rather unusual mousse to serve on special occasions. I have made it for Easter lunch when it seems particularly appropriate with its theme of chocolate.

8 ounces semisweet chocolate,
broken into pieces

1 tablespoon vegetable shortening

FILLING

6 ounces semisweet chocolate,
broken into pieces

2 egg yolks

1 tablespoon Kirsch

1/2 cup heavy cream

1/2 cup light cream

TOPPING

8 ounces fresh strawberries, hulled and
halved **or** quartered

3 tablespoons strawberry jam, sieved

1 tablespoon Kirsch

1 ounce chocolate, broken into small pieces

1/2 cup heavy cream

Use either a deep 6 inch square cake pan or a 7 inch square pan about 2 inches deep. Line it with a large piece of heavy duty foil cut in the corners. Ensure that there is enough foil above the top of the pan to pull the set chocolate out (see below).

Melt the chocolate with the vegetable shortening (page 10), pour two-thirds into the pan, then turn and tilt the pan to give an even coating over the sides and base. Allow to set, then repeat with the remaining chocolate and leave to set for about 30 minutes, or until it is quite hard. Remove from the pan by pulling the foil lining carefully. Peel the foil away from the chocolate case gently.

To make the filling, melt the chocolate (page 10), remove from the heat and beat in the egg yolks and Kirsch. Whip together the light and heavy creams until thick, then fold in the chocolate mixture. Pour into the prepared chocolate case and chill in a refrigerator until set.

Arrange the strawberries in the center of the case, on top of the filling. Put the jam into a small pan, stir in the Kirsch and bring to the boil. Remove from the heat and allow to cool slightly. Spoon the topping over the strawberries; take care not to allow the hot jam to run to the edge of the chocolate case, or it will melt it. Leave for about 5 minutes for the glaze to set. Melt the chocolate (page 10) and allow to cool. Whip the heavy cream until stiff, then beat in the cooled chocolate. Spoon into a pastry bag and pipe neatly round the edge of the case.

Chocolate Creams

The melted chocolate topping is a rather unusual way of presenting this rich custard recipe.

4 egg yolks

¼ cup caster sugar

½ teaspoon vanilla extract

1 cup heavy cream

1 cup light cream

4 ounces semisweet compound chocolate, broken into pieces

2 tablespoons vegetable oil

DECORATION

whipped cream

Butter six ramekins. Beat the egg yolks lightly with the sugar and vanilla extract. Mix together the light and heavy creams and heat to blood temperature. Beat into the egg yolks.

Turn the mixture into the prepared ramkins, cover with foil and stand in a roasting pan containing 1 inch cold water. Bake in a warm oven, 325°F, for about 30 minutes, or until set. Remove from the oven, take out of the water and leave to cool for about 1 hour.

Melt the chocolate with the oil (page 10); this makes it softer for serving. Spoon over the creams, then chill for at least 6 hours. Top each cream with a spoonful of whipped cream before serving.

Serves 6

Chocolate and Almond Layer Pudding

This Polish recipe is extremely rich and quite delicious.

2 ounces semisweet chocolate, broken into pieces

¼ cup unsalted butter

⅓ cup caster sugar

a few drops vanilla extract

½ cup ground almonds

juice of ½ lemon

TOPPING

1 ounce semisweet chocolate, broken into pieces

2 tablespoons butter

½ cup heavy cream

Melt the chocolate (page 10) and cool slightly. Cream the butter, beat in 2 tablespoons sugar and the vanilla extract. Beat until smooth and fluffy, then beat in the chocolate. Turn into a small glass serving bowl and spread evenly. Chill for at least 30 minutes. Mix the almonds with the remaining sugar and lemon juice and spread evenly over the chocolate mixture. Chill while preparing the topping.

Melt the chocolate with the butter (page 10) and remove from the heat. Whip the cream lightly and fold gently into the chocolate. Spoon the topping over the chilled mixture, forming the cream into swirls. Chill in a refrigerator until ready to serve.

Serves 4–6

Apricot Fruit Basket

I made this chocolate basket using a foil container as a mold, approximately 9 × 5 inches and 2 inches deep. To fill the basket, any favorite fruit in season can be used as an alternative to apricots. Apricot, peach or rose leaves, washed and dried, make a pretty decoration if placed round the edge of the basket. If you do not wish to make the handle, use the extra chocolate to make the basket a little thicker.

*7 ounces milk chocolate **or** milk compound chocolate, broken into pieces*

1½ pounds fresh apricots, halved and pitted

sugar

4 tablespoons white wine

1 cup heavy cream

Melt the chocolate (page 10), and use all but about 3 tablespoons to coat the inside of a foil container evenly (see above); use about a third of the melted chocolate at a time, so that it sets quickly. Leave to set in a cool place for at least 30 minutes.

To make the handle, spoon the remainder of the chocolate either into a wax paper pastry bag or into a nylon pastry bag fitted with a small writing tip; (keep the bowl used for melting the chocolate over the pan of hot water). Draw a circle, about ½ inch smaller than the width of the foil dish, on a piece of wax paper or non-stick silicon paper. Pipe a simple trellis pattern round this circle; the easiest one is one wavy line followed by a second wavy line in the opposite direction on top. Leave to set, then carefully cut into two semi-circles, using a sharp knife. Brush the smooth side of one of these with the chocolate remaining in the bowl (you only need a very little), then place the second semi-circle on top, again smooth side down. Leave to set.

Put half the apricots into a blender or food processor, and purée with the sugar and white wine. Whip the cream until it just holds its shape, then carefully fold in the apricot purée.

When the chocolate in the container is quite hard, loosen the foil very gently, and peel away from the chocolate. Spoon the apricot fool into the chocolate case. Arrange the remaining apricot halves on the top, piling them up to look like fruit in a basket. Place the handle in position, pressing it gently into the fool. Decorate with fruit leaves, if liked.

Serves 6–8

Avocado Fool

This is a recipe from the South Pacific.

2 large, ripe avocados, peeled and seeded
juice of 2 limes
2 tablespoons confectioners sugar
2 tablespoons brandy
½ cup heavy cream
3 ounces milk chocolate, grated coarsely

Mash the avocados or purée in a blender or food processor with the lime juice and sugar, then add the brandy. Whip the cream until it holds its shape, then fold in the avocado purée. Taste, adding a little extra sugar if necessary, then turn into four individual bowls or glasses. Sprinkle the chocolate over the fools before serving.

Serves 4

Chocolate Chip Meringue Nests

I have suggested using frozen raspberries so that the dessert can be made at any time of year, but when fresh raspberries are in season, simply spread the bases of the meringue nests with whipped cream and top with the fresh fruit.

2 egg whites
½ cup caster sugar
2 ounces semisweet compound chocolate, grated

FILLING
12 ounces frozen raspberries, thawed
1 tablespoon cornstarch
1 tablespoon sugar
4 tablespoons whipped cream

Draw four circles, each 4 inches in diameter, on a piece of non-stick silicon paper. Oil both sides lightly and place on a cookie sheet. Beat the egg whites until they form stiff peaks, then beat in half the sugar, 1 teaspoon at a time until the mixture is stiff and shiny. Fold in the remainder of the sugar with the chocolate. Divide the meringue mixture between the four circles, building up the sides, so that a 'nest' is formed. Bake in a very cool oven, 250°F, for about 2 hours or until quite dry. Remove from the oven, leave to cool, then peel off the paper carefully. Place on a plate.

To make the filling, drain the raspberries and blend the juice with the cornstarch in a small pan. Add the sugar and bring to the boil, stirring all the time, until thickened. Stir in the raspberries, remove from the heat and leave to cool.

Up to 1 hour before serving, fill the nests with the raspberry mixture and top each one with a spoonful of whipped cream. Chill until ready to serve.

Serves 4

Hazelnut and Orange Torte

2 eggs, separated
¾ cup caster sugar
3 ounces semisweet chocolate, broken into pieces
½ cup butter
½ cup hazelnuts, chopped
2 tablespoons Cointreau
½ cup orange juice
24 ladyfingers
½ cup heavy cream

Oil a cookie sheet lightly and line with non-stick silicon paper. Beat the egg whites until stiff, then beat in ½ cup of the sugar, 1 teaspoon at a time, until the mixture is stiff and shiny. Put in a pastry bag fitted with a large rose tip, and pipe small meringues, about 1½ inches in diameter, to make about 20. Bake in a very cool oven, 250°F, for about 2 hours or until the meringues are crisp. Remove from the oven and leave to cool.

Butter a 2 pound loaf pan lightly and line with non-stick silicon paper. Melt the chocolate (page 10), remove from the heat and cool slightly. Cream together the butter and remaining sugar until light and fluffy, then beat in the chocolate and hazelnuts. Mix the Cointreau with the orange juice. Dip each ladyfinger into the orange mixture for a few seconds, then arrange one-third of them on the base of the pan, sugar side outwards. Spread with half the chocolate mixture. Repeat for the next layer, and finish with a layer of ladyfingers. Cover with a piece of foil, and place a weight on top. Chill in a refrigerator for at least 2 hours, then remove from the pan. Whip the cream until stiff and spread over the cake. Decorate with the meringues.

Serves 6–8

The Chocolate Mousse
Chocolate and Raspberry Layer Mousse (page 69), Chocolate and Crème de Menthe Mousse (page 67), Bitter Chocolate and Orange Mousse (page 67) **and** *Almond Mousse (page 68)*

OVERLEAF LEFT   Chocolate and Strawberry Bombe (page 85)
OVERLEAF RIGHT   Marbled Ice (page 83), Mocha Ice Cream (page 82) **and** *Chocolate Chip Brown Bread Ice Cream (page 83)*

Tia Maria Soufflé

Cold soufflés are very elegant and not difficult to make.

1 envelope powdered gelatin
4 tablespoons cold water
1½ cups milk
3 eggs, separated
¼ cup caster sugar
1 teaspoon vanilla extract
2 tablespoons flour, sifted
8 ounces semisweet chocolate, broken into small pieces
4 tablespoons Tia Maria
1 cup whipping cream

DECORATION

whipped cream
*chocolate leaves **or** horns (page 13)*

Make a collar for a 1½ pint soufflé dish, using a piece of double wax or non-stick silicon paper; the collar should stand at least 4 inches above the rim of the soufflé dish. Brush one side of the piece of paper with oil or butter, wrap round the soufflé dish and tie in position with string.

Sprinkle the gelatin over the water in a bowl and leave to soften for 5 minutes. Pour the milk into a pan and bring to the boil. Beat the egg yolks lightly with the sugar and vanilla extract, then beat in the flour. Pour over the boiling milk, stirring well. Return the mixture to the pan and bring to the boil, stirring all the time, then cook for 2–3 minutes. Remove from the heat and stir in the softened gelatin; leave until dissolved. Add the chocolate and stir until melted. Stir in the Tia Maria. Cover with clingfilm and leave to cool.

Whip the cream until it forms soft peaks, then beat the egg whites until stiff. Fold, first, the cream and then the egg whites into the chocolate custard. Turn the mixture into the prepared dish. Chill in a refrigerator for at least 2 hours.

Before serving, peel off the paper collar carefully, easing it off with a knife. Decorate the top of the soufflé with piped cream and chocolate leaves or horns.

Serves 6

A Selection of Drinks
Coffee Choco (page 91), Crunchy Peppermint Milk Shake (page 93), Iced Chocolate (page 93) **and** *Caribbean Chocolate (page 92)*

Marbled Savarin

This is an ideal dessert for a buffet party and one that can be made all the year round. Use whatever fruit is in season, such as pears, cherries, peaches and strawberries; choose only ripe perfect fruit, and peel, pit and slice as necessary. If catering for smaller numbers, use half quantities and bake in a 7 inch ring pan.

¾ cup butter
1 cup milk
1 teaspoon sugar
2½ teaspoons dried yeast
2¾ cups flour
a pinch of salt
3 eggs, beaten
¼ cup cocoa powder

SYRUP AND FILLING

3 cups sugar
2 cups water
½ cup dark rum
2 pounds prepared fresh fruit (see above)

Grease and flour a 9 inch ring pan. Melt the butter in a pan, then leave to cool. Heat the milk to blood temperature, then pour into a bowl. Stir in the sugar and sprinkle with the yeast. Leave in a warm place for 10 minutes or until frothy. Sift together 2½ cups of the flour with the salt into a mixing bowl. Make a hollow in the center, pour in the yeast mixture and the eggs, and mix well with a wooden spoon to make a smooth dough. Beat in the cooled butter, and beat for a further 2–3 minutes. Divide the mixture in half. Sift the remaining flour into one half and the cocoa into the other half. Beat both batters until smooth.

Put alternate spoonfuls of the mixtures into the prepared pan. Cover with a piece of oiled clingfilm and put into a warm place for about 40 minutes, or until the dough has risen almost to the top of the pan. Bake in a hot oven, 425°F, for about 25 minutes, or until golden-brown and firm. Cool in the pan for 5 minutes, then turn out on to a wire rack with a plate underneath.

Make the syrup while the savarin is cooking. Put the sugar into a pan with the water and stir over low heat until the sugar has dissolved. Bring to the boil, then remove from the heat and stir in the rum.

While the savarin is still hot, prick it all over with a fine skewer and pour over the warm rum syrup, a little at a time. When all the syrup has been used, pour any which has drained on to the plate back into the pan. Pour over the savarin again. Repeat until only about ½ cup is left. Carefully place the savarin on a serving plate. Mix the remaining syrup with the fruit, and spoon this into the center of the savarin. Serve with whipped cream.

Serves 12

Crackolate Cheesecake

The base of this cheesecake is the ever-popular crackolate mixture, which is normally made in small paper cake cases. Made with rice krispies as here, rather than with cornflakes, it makes an unusual and delicious base for an uncooked cheesecake.

¼ cup butter

2 tablespoons corn syrup

2 tablespoons granulated sugar

2 tablespoons cocoa powder

¾ cup rice krispies

FILLING

¾ pound strawberries hulled

¾ pound cottage cheese

1 envelope powdered gelatin

4 tablespoons cold water

2 eggs, separated

⅓ cup caster sugar

grated rind of 1 lemon

½ cup whipping cream

DECORATION

½ cup whipping cream

chocolate leaves (page 13)

Lightly oil a loose-bottomed 8 inch cake pan. Put the butter, syrup, sugar and cocoa into a pan and stir over low heat until the butter has melted and the sugar dissolved. Remove from the heat and stir in the rice krispies. Spread evenly over the bottom of the prepared pan and leave to set for 30 minutes.

To make the filling, rub the strawberries with the cottage cheese through a sieve, or purée in a blender or food processor. Sprinkle the gelatin over the cold water in a bowl and leave to soften for 5 minutes. Stand over a pan of simmering water and leave until the gelatin has dissolved. Remove from the heat and allow to cool slightly. Beat the egg yolks with the sugar and lemon rind until thick and creamy. Beat the egg whites until stiff. Whip the cream until stiff. Stir the strawberry and cheese purée into the egg yolk mixture, stir in the gelatin, then fold in the cream and finally the egg whites. Turn into the prepared pan on top of the chocolate base and leave to set for at least 2 hours.

To serve, carefully push the cake out of the pan from the base. Loosen the base with a spatula and transfer to a serving plate. Whip the cream, and spread evenly over the top of the cake. Decorate with the chocolate leaves.

Serves 6–8

Chocolate and Ginger Cheesecake

7 ounces ginger cookies

1/3 cup butter

1 tablespoon Demerara sugar

FILLING

4 ounces semisweet chocolate,
broken into pieces

1/2 pound cream cheese

2 tablespoons ginger syrup

3 tablespoons light cream

2 eggs, separated

3 pieces preserved stem ginger,
chopped finely

DECORATION

4 tablespoons whipped cream (approx)

1–2 pieces preserved stem ginger, sliced

Crush the cookies with a rolling-pin between the folds of a dish towel, or use a food processor. Melt the butter in a small pan, remove from the heat and stir in the cookies and sugar. Press into a 8–9 inch flan pan, or dish, and chill.

To make the filling, melt the chocolate (page 10). Remove from the heat. Beat the cream cheese with the ginger syrup and light cream, then beat in the egg yolks, one at a time, followed by the chocolate and ginger. Beat the egg whites until stiff, then fold into the cream cheese mixture.

Turn the mixture into the cookie cases and chill in a refrigerator for at least 1 hour. Decorate with whipped cream, piped or swirled on the top, and small pieces of stem ginger.

Serves 6

Mocha Ice Cream

1/2 cup soft brown sugar

4 tablespoons cocoa powder

2 tablespoons instant coffee granules

1/4 cup butter

5 tablespoons water

2 cups canned evaporated milk

Put the sugar, cocoa, coffee, butter and water into a pan. Heat gently, stirring until melted, then bring to the boil. Leave to cool. Pour the evaporated milk into a large mixing bowl. Beat until thick and frothy and the beater leaves a trail, then beat in the cooled sauce until well blended.

Turn the mixture into a freezer and leave until partially frozen. Remove and beat well. Pour into a freezer container, freeze until firm, then cover.

Serves 6

Note *Evaporated milk can be whipped if it is at room temperature, but it whips better if chilled overnight.*

Chocolate Chip Brown Bread Ice Cream

Most recipes for brown bread ice cream suggest toasting the breadcrumbs before use, so that they give a crisp texture. This is not quite as easy as it sounds, as the crumbs easily burn unless turned frequently. Adding chocolate to the mixture not only enhances the flavor, but also gives a crunchy texture without any of the bother.

1 cup heavy cream
½ cup light cream
2 eggs, separated
½ cup confectioners sugar, sifted
1 cup wholewheat breadcrumbs
2 ounces semisweet chocolate, grated coarsely **or** chopped finely

Lightly whip the heavy and light creams together until they hold their shape. Beat the egg yolks and confectioners sugar until thick and creamy, then stir in the breadcrumbs and chocolate. Fold into the whipped cream. Beat the egg whites until they form stiff peaks, then fold into the cream. Turn the mixture into a 1 quart freezer container and freeze for 2–3 hours until firm.

Serves 6

Marbled Ice

1 cup milk
⅓ cup caster sugar
4 egg yolks
1 cup heavy cream
½ teaspoon vanilla extract
3 ounces semisweet chocolate, broken into pieces

Heat the milk with the sugar to blood temperature. Beat the egg yolks, then pour over the hot milk, beating all the time. Return the mixture to the pan and stir over very low heat until the custard thickens; take great care not to curdle the mixture. Remove from the heat, cover the pan with clingfilm and leave to cool.

Whip the cream very lightly; it should be just slightly thickened. Beat the cooled custard and fold into the cream. Pour half the mixture into a plastic container and stir in the vanilla extract.

Melt the chocolate (page 10), and stir into the remaining mixture. Carefully pour the chocolate mixture in a zigzag pattern over the vanilla ice. Stir very lightly with a spoon to give a marbled appearance. Freeze for at least 4 hours.

Serves 6–8

Chocolate Tutti Frutti Bombe

This makes a spectacular dessert for a dinner party, especially when served at the table flaming.
Any left over can be stored in a freezer.

½ pound compound chocolate,
broken into pieces

3 eggs, separated

½ cup confectioners sugar, sifted

1 cup heavy cream

1 cup candied cherries, chopped

1 cup dried apricots, chopped

1 cup candied peel, chopped

1 cup blanched almonds, chopped

5 tablespoons brandy **or** dark rum

Put a 2 quart dessert bowl (a plastic one is ideal) in the freezer for a few minutes. Melt the chocolate (page 10). Remove the bowl and pour in the chocolate. Roll it round and round until the inside is coated evenly. Leave to set.

Beat the egg yolks with 2 tablespoons of the sugar until thick and creamy. Beat the egg whites until stiff, then beat in the remaining sugar, 1 teaspoon at a time. Beat in the egg yolks gradually. Whip the cream lightly. Fold all the fruit and nuts into the egg mixture, then fold in the cream. Turn the mixture into the prepared bowl. If the ice cream level does not quite reach the level of the chocolate, neaten off with a sharp knife. Any excess chocolate can be chopped and stirred into the ice cream mixture. Cover the bowl and freeze for at least 4 hours or until quite firm.

To turn the dessert out, dip into a bowl of very hot water for about 1 minute and invert on to a plate; replace in the freezer. About 30 minutes before serving, place on a serving plate and put in the refrigerator; (do not use the plate that has been in the freezer as this will prevent the alcohol from igniting.)

Put the brandy or rum into a small pan and heat gently, then pour over the dessert, and ignite.

Serves 8–12

Note   *It does not matter if the chocolate covering is not smoothly coated, as it will not be visible once the bombe is filled with ice cream.*

Chocolate and Strawberry Bombe

CHOCOLATE ICE CREAM
4 egg yolks

⅓ cup caster sugar

2 cups light cream

3 ounces semisweet chocolate,
broken into small pieces

STRAWBERRY ICE CREAM
¾ pound fresh **or** frozen strawberries,
thawed

4 egg yolks

½ cup caster sugar

1½ cups light cream

DECORATION (optional)
whipped cream

fresh strawberries **or** chocolate curls
(page 12) **or** leaves (page 13)

Beat the egg yolks and sugar in a bowl over a pan of simmering water until thick and creamy. Heat the cream in a small pan to blood temperature. Stir into the egg yolks and cook over low heat, stirring all the time, until the mixture thickens. Remove from the heat and stir in the chocolate until melted. Pour into a 1½ quart bowl and leave to cool for about 1 hour. Put a 1½ pint bowl in the center and place enough weights inside to bring the mixture level with the top of the bowl. Freeze for at least 2 hours or until firm.

Pour a little hot water into the inner bowl, and as soon as the ice cream round the edge starts to melt, remove it carefully. Return the ice cream to the freezer.

To make the strawberry ice cream, rub the strawberries through a sieve or purée in a blender or food processor. Using the egg yolks, sugar and cream, make the ice cream mixture as for the chocolate ice cream . Remove from the heat and stir in the strawberry purée. Cool for about 1 hour. Pour the strawberry ice cream into the cavity left in the center of the chocolate ice cream, and freeze for a further 2–3 hours until quite firm.

To turn out, quickly dip thc bowl into a bowl of very hot water for a few seconds and invert on to a serving plate. Either serve the bombe as it is, or decorate with whipped cream and fresh strawberries, or chocolate curls or leaves.

Serves 8

Lemon Sorbet with Raspberry Sauce

If you use shop lemon sorbet, as I suggest, you can present an immaculate and delicious dessert with very little difficulty. Home-made sorbet can also, of course, be used.

1 pint carton lemon sorbet

6 ounces semisweet chocolate, broken into pieces

2 tablespoons vegetable oil

¾ pound frozen raspberries, thawed

¼ cup confectioners sugar

Using either a small ice-cream scoop, or a dessert-spoon, form the sorbet into 18 balls. Place on a piece of non-stick silicon or wax paper on a tray and put into a freezer for about 10 minutes to harden.

Melt the chocolate with the oil (page 10) and allow to cool slightly. Spoon a little chocolate carefully over each ball of sorbet, coating them evenly. Return the tray to the freezer for at least 15 minutes.

Reserve six raspberries for decoration. Rub the remaining raspberries through a sieve or purée in a blender or food processor (then sieve the purée to remove the seeds). Stir in the confectioners sugar. To serve, divide the sauce between six plates, top with three balls of chocolate-covered sorbet and decorate each one with a raspberry.

Serves 6

VARIATION   *Different flavors of sorbet, and combinations of flavors, can be used.*

Layered Log Ice Cream

A marvelous way of turning a block of commercially made ice cream into an elegant dinner party dessert with the minimum of time, effort and money.

2 teaspoons instant coffee granules

1 tablespoon Tia Maria **or** rum

½ cup hazelnuts

½ cup shredded coconut

1 heaping tablespoon chocolate spread

1 tablespoon milk **or** coconut milk

2 quarts vanilla ice cream

3 ounces semisweet chocolate,
broken into pieces

Dissolve the coffee in the Tia Maria or rum. Toast the hazelnuts under a moderate broiler for a few minutes. Remove from the heat and, when cool enough to handle, rub them together until the skins come off. Replace the nuts under the broiler and cook until golden-brown, taking care that they do not burn, then chop them very finely by hand or with a blender or food processor.

Lightly toast the coconut, making sure it all becomes evenly golden and does not burn. Blend the chocolate spread with the milk or coconut milk to form a smooth paste.

Divide the ice cream into three portions; leave two in the freezer and place the third in a mixing bowl. Chop this roughly into about six portions and leave to soften for about 5 minutes. Pour in the coffee mixture, then beat well (preferably with an electric beater). Turn into a 2 pound loaf pan, spread evenly over the base, then replace in the freezer for about 10 minutes until quite firm.

Remove a second portion of ice cream, chop and soften as before and beat in the hazelnuts. Spread this over the coffee ice cream and leave to harden in the freezer.

Finally, beat the chocolate spread and coconut milk into the last portion of ice cream, spread over the hazelnut mixture and chill for at least 1 hour.

To turn the ice cream out, quickly dip the pan into a bowl of very hot water for a few seconds, and invert on to a plate. Replace in the freezer for 5 minutes. Melt the chocolate and drizzle all over the top and sides of the ice cream (page 13). Replace in the freezer until ready to serve.

Serves 8

Chocolate Terrine with Cherry Sauce

This is a wonderful rich chocolate dessert. I have deliberately made a fairly large quantity as it is a marvelous standby for the freezer and you can just cut off a slice or two when you want it. Beware, however, it is very rich so you will not want much!

½ pound semisweet chocolate, broken into pieces

1 cup unsalted butter

½ cup confectioners sugar

½ cup cocoa powder

4 egg yolks

½ cup granulated sugar

½ cup water

1 cup heavy cream

*1 cup pitted bing cherries (fresh **or** frozen), chopped roughly*

SAUCE

*1 pound pitted bing cherries (fresh **or** frozen)*

1¼ cups water

½ cup sugar

2 tablespoons cornstarch

4 tablespoons Kirsch (optional)

Butter a 3 pound loaf pan. Melt the chocolate (page 10). Remove from the heat and leave to cool slightly. Cream the butter until light and fluffy. Sift the confectioners sugar and cocoa together and beat into the butter alternately with the chocolate. Beat the egg yolks lightly in a separate bowl. Put the sugar and water into a small, heavy-based pan and stir over low heat until the sugar has dissolved. Boil rapidly to 225°F on a candy thermometer, (thread stage). Beat into the egg yolks, a little at a time, and beat to a mousse-like consistency. Beat slowly into the butter mixture. Whip the cream lightly, then fold into the chocolate mixture. Fold in the cherries last. Turn into the prepared pan and freeze for at least 6 hours or until firm. Serve each portion with about 2 tablespoons of hot cherry sauce.

To make the cherry sauce, put the cherries, all but 3 tablespoons of the water and the sugar into a pan, and bring to the boil. Blend the cornstarch with the remaining water, stir into the pan and bring back to the boil, stirring all the time. Remove from the heat and stir in the Kirsch, if used.

Terrine serves 12–16
Sauce serves 8–10

VARIATION   *Serve the Terrine with warm Chocolate Fudge Sauce (page 91) instead of the Cherry Sauce.*

Sauces and Drinks

Chocolate sauce is the perfect accompaniment for ice cream and numerous other desserts, both hot and cold. Use any of the recipes in this chapter and see how easy it is to transform a simple dessert into something quite special.

If you want to make a chocolate sauce which is not too sweet, use unsweetened chocolate as this produces a really excellent rich sauce. Try any of these recipes using unsweetened chocolate, and add just a very little extra sugar.

Chocolate milk shakes are always popular and for these you can use either a commercial syrup or instant chocolate milk mix. The homemade syrup on page 93 is, however, extremely useful as it keeps in a refrigerator for weeks.

Rich Chocolate Sauce (1)

Since this sauce can be served at any temperature, it is ideal for most desserts, but especially profiteroles and ice cream. If you are serving it cold, add about 3 tablespoons light cream to keep it at a pouring consistency.

1 heaping tablespoon cocoa powder
¾ cup canned evaporated milk
3 ounces semisweet chocolate, broken into small pieces

Beat together the cocoa and evaporated milk in a small pan. Put over low heat and bring to boiling point. Remove from the heat and stir in the chocolate. Return to low heat and continue stirring until the chocolate has melted.

Serves 4–6

Rich Chocolate Sauce (2)

A richer sauce than the previous recipe.

½ cup butter
½ cup caster sugar
a pinch of salt
2 tablespoons dark rum
½ cup cocoa powder
½ cup heavy cream
1 teaspoon vanilla extract

Melt the butter in a small pan. Stir in the sugar, salt, rum and the cocoa. Mix well over low heat. Add the cream and bring to the boil. Simmer very gently for 5 minutes. Remove from the heat and add the vanilla extract. Serve hot or cold.

Serves 6–8

Chocolate and Orange Sauce

½ cup fresh orange juice
grated rind of 1 orange
2 tablespoons butter
1 cup milk chocolate chips

Heat the orange juice and rind, and the butter in a small pan and, when the butter has melted, bring to boiling point. Remove from the heat, stir in the chocolate and return to the heat, stirring all the time. When the chocolate has melted, boil for about 1 minute.

Serves 4–6

Note   *Orange juice from a carton can be used instead of the fresh orange juice and rind , but this does not give such a strong orange flavor to the sauce.*

Charlotte's Peppermint Sauce

A very sweet sauce, deemed 'delicious' by my eleven-year-old niece. Perfect for ice cream.

3 ounces chocolate-covered peppermint creams
½ cup light cream

Break each chocolate in half and melt in a bowl over a pan of hot water. Remove from the heat and gradually stir in the cream. Serve warm or cold.

Serves 4–6

Chocolate Fudge Sauce

The sugar may be left out of this sauce if you prefer it less sweet, but its omission will tend to make the butter separate out. To rectify this, let the sauce cool a little, or leave until cold, and beat just before serving. If you plan to serve it cold, add about 3 tablespoons light cream to keep it at a pouring consistency.

¼ cup unsalted butter
½ cup milk
2 tablespoons caster sugar
4 ounces semisweet chocolate, broken into small pieces

Put the butter, milk and sugar into a small pan and bring to the boil. Remove from the heat and add the chocolate. Stir until the chocolate has melted, then return to the heat and boil rapidly for 2 minutes.

Serves 4–6

Bitter Fudge Sauce

⅓ cup butter
2 ounces unsweetened chocolate
¼ cup granulated sugar
½ cup light cream

Put all the ingredients into a small pan. Put over a gentle heat, stirring frequently until the butter and chocolate have melted. Bring to the boil for about 1 minute, stirring all the time, until a smooth, thick sauce is obtained. Serve hot.

Serves 4–6

VARIATION   *Flavor the sauce with rum, brandy or any liqueur. Add after the sauce has boiled.*

Coffee Choco

1½ cups milk
1½ cups water
1½ tablespoons instant coffee granules
1 tablespoon instant cocoa powder
4 chocolate flakes bars

Heat the milk and water to just below boiling point. Blend in the coffee and cocoa, and mix well. Pour into glasses and put a chocolate flake into each glass.

Serves 4

Rum Toddy

An ideal warmer for a cold winter's day.

1/2 ounce semisweet chocolate, broken into pieces
1/2 cup milk
1 tablespoon dark rum
1 heaping teaspoon whipped cream
a little grated nutmeg

Put the chocolate and milk into a small pan and bring to the boil, stirring once or twice. Remove from the heat and beat in the rum. Pour into a small cup or glass. Top with the cream and sprinkle with the nutmeg.

Serves 1

Caribbean Chocolate

1 cup milk
1 1/2 tablespoons instant chocolate milk mix
a good pinch of ground nutmeg
a good pinch of ground allspice
a good pinch of ground cinnamon
1 tablespoon whipped cream
instant chocolate milk mix

Put the milk, chocolate and spices into a pan and bring to the boil. Remove from the heat, beat well and pour into a mug. Top with the whipped cream and sprinkle with a little extra chocolate milk mix.

Serves 1

Quickie Milk Shake

3 heaping tablespoons vanilla ice cream
2 tablespoons instant chocolate milk mix
1/2 cup milk

Blend all the ingredients in a blender or food processor for about 30 seconds. Serve immediately.

Serves 1

Crunchy Peppermint Milk Shake

The hamburger chains have turned every child into a milk shake connoisseur. This one should prove very popular.

2 tablespoons semisweet chocolate bits
3 tablespoons chocolate ice cream
½ cup cold milk
¼ teaspoon peppermint extract

Put the chocolate into a blender or food processor. Add all the remaining ingredients and blend for 30 seconds until well mixed and frothy. Serve at once.

Serves 1

Iced Chocolate

Perfect for a hot summer's day.

1 cup milk
½ cup light cream
3 tablespoons Chocolate Syrup
8 ice cubes (approx)

Beat together the milk, cream and syrup. Put the ice cubes into a jug, pour over the chocolate, and serve.

Serves 4

VARIATION   *Top with small scoops of ice cream.*

Chocolate Syrup

This syrup is particularly useful as it can be kept in a covered container in a refrigerator for weeks. Use as a base for milk shakes, or pour over ice cream as a sauce and then with a little milk.

1½ cups soft brown sugar
1 cup cocoa powder
¼ teaspoon salt
1 cup water
2 teaspoons vanilla extract

Put all the ingredients, except the vanilla extract, into a pan, mix well and bring to the boil. Cook gently for 5 minutes, stirring frequently. Remove from the heat, leave to cool, then stir in the vanilla extract. Cover and chill in a refrigerator until required.

The
Chocolate Classics

Most Western countries boast a 'classic' chocolate dish, many of which are closely identified with the food of that country. Think of Sacher Torte and you think of Austria, Schwarzwälderkirschtorte signifies Germany, Devil's Food Cake means the United States. These dishes are not just among the best chocolate recipes in the world, but some of the best of all recipes in the world, and I can certainly find a number of my all-time favorites among them. The following is just such a selection and to my mind, epitomizes what chocolate cookery is all about.

Classic Cakes
Scwarzwälderkirschtorte (page 102),
Sacher Torte (page 104) **and** *Dobos Torte*
(page 101)

Mole de Guajolote

The exact translation of Mole de Guajolote is Turkey with Mole Sauce which is a very well known Mexican dish served on feast days and holidays. An authentic mole sauce is, however, extremely complicated to make, requiring about three different kinds of chillies as well as special green tomatoes and other ingredients. I have, therefore, simplified the recipe considerably, using ingredients which are readily available but have not detracted from a delicious authentic end result.

1 × 3 pound chicken
salt
1 teaspoon black peppercorns
2 onions
2 tablespoons oil
2 green chillies, deseeded and finely chopped
1 clove of garlic, crushed
4 cloves
¼ teaspoon whole cumin seeds
½ teaspoon ground cinnamon
2 tablespoons ground almonds
2 tablespoons sesame seeds
½ cup corn-meal
1 × 15 ounce can tomatoes
1 ounce semisweet chocolate,
broken into pieces

Skin the chicken, bone it and cut the flesh into 1 inch cubes. Put the chicken skin and bones into a saucepan, with 1 teaspoon salt, the peppercorns and 1 onion, roughly chopped. Cover with cold water and bring to the boil, then simmer gently for 45 minutes–1 hour.

Heat the oil in a large skillet and gently fry the second onion, finely chopped, the chillies and garlic for 8 minutes. Remove from the heat and add all the remaining ingredients. Pour in 1 cup of the chicken stock. Return to the heat, bring to the boil, stirring all the time, then cover and cook over very low heat for 20 minutes, stirring frequently to prevent it from sticking to the pan. Rub through a sieve or purée in a blender or food processor, then return to the pan.

Strain the remaining stock and gently poach the chicken pieces in it for about 10 minutes, then remove with a slotted spoon. Re-heat the mole sauce, add the chicken pieces and simmer for about 5 minutes. Season to taste.

Serve with boiled rice and tortillas, if available.

Serves 4

Saint Emilion au Chocolat (page 109)

Lepre con Agrodolce

Agrodolce is a classic Italian sauce, the origins of which can be traced back to the Romans. It is almost always served with game, such as hare, wild boar, wild duck and venison. The Spanish, who are great game eaters, also cook both hare and partridge in a chocolate sauce.

1 hare, skinned and disjointed
1 cup red wine vinegar
1 cup water
½ cup flour
salt and freshly ground black pepper
2 tablespoons butter
2 tablespoons oil
½ cup Canadian bacon, chopped
1 cup red wine
1 cup stock
a sprig of thyme

SAUCE
¼ cup sugar
½ cup red wine vinegar
1 clove of garlic, crushed
1 ounce unsweetened chocolate
1 tablespoon raisins

Put the hare pieces in a bowl. Mix together the wine vinegar and water, pour over the hare and leave to marinate for 4 hours, turning from time to time.

Remove the hare from the marinade and dry thoroughly. Coat with the flour seasoned with salt and pepper. Heat the butter and oil in a skillet. Add the bacon and fry gently for 5 minutes. Remove and put to one side. Fry the pieces of hare, a few at a time, until brown. Put all the hare and the bacon back in the pan. Pour over the wine and stock, add the thyme, cover and cook gently for 1½ hours.

To make the sauce, put the sugar and vinegar into a small, heavy-based pan. Stir over low heat until the sugar has dissolved. Bring to the boil and boil rapidly to 345°F on a candy thermometer (caramel stage). Remove from the heat and stir in the garlic and the chocolate. When the chocolate has melted, strain in 1½ cups of the stock from cooking the hare. Replace over gentle heat and simmer for about 5 minutes. Place the pieces of hare on a serving plate and pour over the chocolate sauce.

Serves 6

Brownies

There must be more different recipes for Brownies than there are states in the Union, but the one essential for a good Brownie is that it must have a soft and chewy center.

⅓ cup butter
2 ounces semisweet chocolate
¾ cup soft brown sugar
¾ cup self-rising flour, sifted
2 eggs, beaten
½ cup walnuts, chopped roughly

Grease and flour a shallow 8 inch square cake pan. Melt the chocolate and butter (page 10). Remove from the heat and stir in the sugar. Beat in the flour and eggs until smooth. Stir in the walnuts.

Pour the mixture into the prepared pan and bake in a medium oven, 350°F, for 35–40 minutes until well risen and firm to the touch; the inside should be slightly soft and cracked on the surface. Cool slightly before cutting into squares or bars.

Makes 16

Florentines

Florentines, often so inviting in the patîsserie, are sometimes slightly disappointing when eaten because inferior chocolate has been used for coating them. A good quality chocolate makes all the difference.

¼ cup butter
¼ cup caster sugar
¼ cup flour, sifted
½ cup blanched almonds, chopped
¼ cup candied cherries, chopped
¼ cup candied peel, chopped
4 ounces semisweet chocolate, broken into pieces

Line two cookie sheets with non-stick silicon paper. Put the butter and sugar into a small pan and heat gently until melted. Remove from the heat and stir in the flour with the almonds, cherries and peel.

Drop spoonfuls of the mixture, well apart, on to the prepared cookie sheets. Bake in a medium oven, 350°F, for about 10 minutes until golden-brown. Leave to cool on the cookie sheets until set, then lift on to a cooling rack.

Melt the chocolate (page 10). Spread over the smooth sides of the cookies. Before it sets, mark in wavy lines with the prongs of a fork.

Makes about 8

Devil's Food Cake

Undoubtedly one of America's best-known cakes for which there are countless recipes. Yet few things are more tempting than the sight of a slice of rich dark chocolate cake filled and topped with thick white frosting – Devil's Food Cake is a very apt name.

½ cup milk
1 cup soft brown sugar
1 cup cocoa powder
½ cup butter
2 eggs, beaten
2 cups flour
1 teaspoon bicarbonate of soda

FROSTING

2 cups granulated sugar
½ cup water
2 egg whites

Grease and line an 8 inch baking pan. Put the milk, sugar, cocoa and butter in a pan. Heat gently, stirring until melted and smooth. Leave to cool. Beat in the eggs until smooth. Sift together the flour with the bicarbonate of soda and beat into the chocolate mixture to give a smooth thick batter.

Pour the batter into the prepared pan and bake in a warm oven, 325°F, for about 1 hour until risen and firm. Allow to cool in the pan for 5 minutes, then turn out on to a wire rack and leave to cool. When cold, split into three rounds.

To make the frosting, put the sugar and water in a small pan. Stir over low heat to dissolve the sugar, then boil to 240°F on a candy thermometer (soft ball stage). Beat the egg whites in a large mixing bowl until very stiff. When the syrup has reached the required temperature, allow the bubbles to subside, then pour on to the beaten egg whites, beating all the time. Continue beating until the frosting thickens and stands in soft peaks. Use at once to sandwich together the rounds of cake. Spread the remaining frosting over the cake, swirling with a spatula and pulling up into peaks. Leave to set for 30 minutes.

Dobos Torte

The unusual, and distinctive, part about Hungary's most famous cake is the caramel spread over the top of it. This not only makes it look very attractive, but also adds a subtle flavor.

4 eggs, separated

1½ cups caster sugar

1 cup ground hazelnuts (see **Note**)

FILLING

4 ounces semisweet chocolate, broken into pieces

½ cup unsalted butter

½ cup confectioners sugar, sifted

TOPPING

¾ cup granulated sugar

3 tablespoons water

a few whole hazelnuts

Grease and line two 7 inch layer-cake pans, preferably with non-stick silicon paper. Beat the egg yolks and sugar until thick and creamy. Beat the egg whites until they form stiff peaks. Fold the hazelnuts and egg whites alternately into the egg yolks.

Divide the mixture between the two pans and bake in a medium oven, 350°F, for 30 minutes or until set. Allow to cool in the pans for 10 minutes, then turn out on to a wire rack and leave to cool.

To make the filling, melt the chocolate (page 10). Cream the butter and confectioners sugar, then beat in the chocolate. Use half of the mixture to sandwich together the two cakes.

To make the topping, put the sugar and water into a small pan and stir over low heat until the sugar has dissolved. Bring to the boil and boil rapidly to 345°F on a candy thermometer (caramel stage). Using an oiled knife, spread the caramel evenly over the top of the cake. While it is still soft, mark into eight pieces with a sharp knife and leave to set.

Put the remaining buttercream into a pastry bag and pipe round the edge of the cake. Decorate with a few whole hazelnuts.

Note *Whole hazelnuts, ground in a blender or food processor can also be used.*

Schwarzwälderkirschtorte

This classic German gâteau, known in translation as Black Forest Cherry Gâteau should be made with black cherries, but their season is fairly short, and even in summer they are not readily available. I have, therefore, suggested using frozen pitted cherries which can be found in many supermarkets and most deep-freeze centers.

5 eggs
1¼ cups caster sugar
1 cup self-rising flour
¼ cup cocoa powder
4 tablespoons vegetable oil

FILLING AND DECORATION

1 pound frozen pitted black cherries, thawed
6 tablespoons Kirsch
1½ cups heavy cream
½ cup confectioners sugar, sifted
2 ounces chocolate caraque (page 12)

Grease and line a 9 inch round cake pan. Beat the eggs and sugar until thick and creamy, and the beater leaves a trail when lifted out of the mixture. Sift in the flour and cocoa and fold into the mixture. Fold in the oil.

Turn the mixture into the prepared pan and bake in a moderately hot oven, 357°F, for about 30 minutes. Allow to cool in the pan for 5 minutes, then turn out on to a wire rack and leave to cool.

To make the filling and decoration, drain the juice from the cherries into a small pan, bring to the boil and boil rapidly until only about 2 tablespoons of syrup are left. Remove from the heat and stir in the cherries and half the Kirsch. Whip the cream until it holds its shape, then fold in the remaining Kirsch and the confectioners sugar.

Split the cake into three rounds. Place the bottom round on a serving plate, spread with some of the cream and half the cherries, place the second round on top, spread with more cream and the rest of the cherries, and then top with the last round. Spread the remaining cream over the cake, bringing it up into swirls. Decorate the top with the chocolate caraque and chill until ready to serve.

Chocolate Mousse Torte

This is a somewhat unusual recipe. Three-quarters of the mixture is first baked; this rises rather like a soufflé, and then sinks in the middle as it cools. The hole in the center is then filled with the remainder of the uncooked mixture.

2 tablespoons dry breadcrumbs

8 ounces semisweet chocolate,
broken into pieces

1 tablespoon instant coffee granules

4 tablespoons water

8 eggs, separated

¾ cup caster sugar

1 teaspoon vanilla extract

DECORATION

½ cup whipping cream

chocolate curls (page 12)

Lightly butter a 9 inch flan pan or ring (approximately 1 quart capacity) and coat with the dry breadcrumbs. Melt the chocolate with the coffee and water (page 10). Remove from the heat. Beat together the egg yolks, sugar and vanilla extract in a large bowl until thick and creamy, then beat in the chocolate. Beat the egg whites until stiff, then fold into the chocolate mixture. Fill the flan pan with about three-quarters of the mixture. Cover the remainder and chill in a refrigerator.

Bake the flan in a medium oven, 350°F, for 25 minutes. Turn off the oven and leave for a further 5 minutes, then remove and leave to cool for 2 hours.

Fill the cavity in the center with the chilled mixture and chill in a refrigerator for 30 minutes. Whip the cream until stiff and spread over the top. Decorate with the chocolate curls.

Serves 6–8

Sacher Torte

Although this cake is named after the founder of the world-renowned Hotel Sacher in Vienna, the original recipe is generally regarded as quite secret.

8 ounces semisweet chocolate,
broken into pieces

1 tablespoon strong black coffee

1 cup butter

1 cup sugar

5 eggs, separated

1½ cups self-rising flour, sifted

FILLING

4 tablespoons apricot jam, sieved

FROSTING

6 ounces semisweet chocolate,
broken into pieces

5 tablespoons strong black coffee

1½ cups confectioners sugar, sifted

Grease and line a 9 inch cake pan. Melt the chocolate with the coffee (page 10) and allow to cool. Cream the butter and sugar until light and fluffy. Beat in the egg yolks, one at a time, then the cooled chocolate. Fold in the flour. Beat the egg whites until they form stiff peaks, then fold gently into the mixture.

Turn the mixture into the prepared pan and bake in a cool oven, 300°F, for 1½ hours. Leave to cool in the pan for 15 minutes, then turn out on to a wire rack and leave to cool. When quite cold, split the cake into two rounds.

To make the filling, warm the apricot jam gently. Spread one round of the cake with most of the apricot jam, sandwich the rounds together, then brush the remainder of the apricot jam all over the cake.

To make the frosting, melt the chocolate with the coffee (page 10). Remove from the heat and beat in the confectioners sugar. Pour the frosting over the cake, spreading it evenly with a spatula dipped in warm water. Leave to set for at least 1 hour. Serve with whipped cream.

Chocolate Eclairs

A simple and well-known chocolate classic.

10 tablespoons flour

a pinch of salt

1/4 cup butter, cut into small pieces

1/2 cup water

2 eggs

1 egg yolk

FILLING AND FROSTING

1 cup heavy cream

1 egg white

1 tablespoon confectioners sugar

6 ounces semisweet chocolate,
broken into pieces

Sift together the flour and salt on to a sheet of wax paper. Put the butter into a pan with the water. Put over gentle heat until the butter has melted, then bring to the boil. Remove the pan from the heat, add the flour all at once and beat well until the mixture forms a soft ball and leaves the sides of the pan clean. If necessary, replace the pan over very low heat. Allow to cool slightly, then beat in the whole eggs and the egg yolk, one at a time, until a very smooth, shiny mixture results.

Put the pastry into a pastry bag fitted with a 1/2 inch plain tip and pipe out 3 inch lengths on to greased cookie sheets; allow plenty of room on the trays for the éclairs to rise and spread.

Bake the éclairs in a moderately hot oven, 400°F for about 25 minutes, or until golden-brown. Remove from the oven, make a couple of slits in the sides of each one to allow the steam to escape and return to the oven for a further 5–10 minutes to dry out. Remove from the oven and leave to cool on a wire rack.

To make the filling, whip the cream until stiff. Beat the egg white until it forms stiff peaks, then beat in the confectioners sugar, 1 teaspoon at a time. Fold into the cream. Make a slit down the side of each éclair and fill with the cream, or pipe it in.

Melt the chocolate (page 10), then pour into a container long enough to be able to dip the top surface of each éclair into the chocolate. Dip the tops of the éclairs into the chocolate, then leave to set.

Makes about 12

Bûche de Noel

France's classic Christmas cake – it freezes well so you can make it several weeks in advance.

4 eggs
1/2 cup caster sugar
3/4 cup self-rising flour
1/4 cup cocoa powder

FILING AND FROSTING
1/2 cup milk
2 egg yolks
6 ounces semisweet chocolate, broken into small pieces
1/2 cup unsalted butter
1/2 cup confectioners sugar, sifted
extra confectioners sugar
holly **or** other Christmas cake decorations

Grease and line a 13 × 9 inch jelly roll pan. Beat the eggs and sugar together until thick and creamy, and the beater leaves a trail when lifted out of the mixture. Sift in the flour and cocoa, and fold in. Turn the mixture into the prepared pan.

Bake in a moderately hot oven, 400°F, for 12–15 minutes or until the cake springs back when pressed lightly. Turn out on to a piece of wax or non-stick silicon paper, dredged with confectioners or caster sugar. Carefully peel off the lining paper, trim off the edges, and roll up the jelly roll, keeping the paper inside the roll. Put to one side and allow to cool.

To make the filling, heat the milk to blood temperature in a small saucepan. Blend the egg yolks in a bowl or the top of a double boiler, and beat in the milk. Stand the mixture over a pan of gently simmering water, and cook, stirring frequently, until the mixture coats the back of a wooden spoon. Add the chocolate, and stir until it has melted, then remove from the heat. Cover the bowl with a piece of clingfilm and leave to cool, stirring from time to time. Cream the butter and beat in the confectioners sugar, then gradually beat in the cooled custard.

Unroll the jelly roll, and spread with a third of the filling. Re-roll and spread the outside of the roll with the remaining frosting.

Using a fork, mark lines on the top of the log, as if for the bark of the tree. Chill in refrigerator for about 1 hour until set, then sprinkle all over with confectioners sugar, and decorate with holly, cake decorations, etc.

Chocolate Chiffon Pie

There are a number of chiffon pies of which chocolate and lemon are the best known.

1½ cups flour

a pinch of salt

⅓ cup butter **or** margarine

cold water

FILLING AND TOPPING

1 envelope powdered gelatin

2 tablespoons cold water

3 eggs, separated

¼ cup caster sugar

4 ounces semisweet chocolate cake covering,
broken into pieces

1 tablespoon cocoa powder

1 teaspoon instant coffee granules

½ cup whipping cream

Sift together the flour and salt. Rub in the butter or margarine until the mixture resembles fine breadcrumbs, then bind with cold water to make a firm dough. Turn on to a floured surface and knead lightly. Roll out and use to line an 8 inch pie plate or pan. Prebake in a moderately hot oven, 375°F, for 20–25 minutes. Leave to cool.

To make the filling, sprinkle the gelatin over the cold water in a bowl. Leave to soften for 5 minutes. Put the egg yolks and sugar into the top of a double boiler or a bowl over a pan of boiling water, and beat until the mixture thickens. Beat in the gelatin and stir until dissolved. Stir in the chocolate, cocoa and coffee granules. Continue stirring until the chocolate has melted. Remove from the heat and allow to cool slightly. Beat the egg whites until they form stiff peaks, then fold into the chocolate mixture.

Turn the mixture into the baked tart shell and chill in a refrigerator for at least 1 hour. Before serving, whip the cream lightly, and spread over the top of the pie.

Serves 4–6

Nègre en Chemise

A superb French recipe, Nègre en Chemise is a very sophisticated steamed dessert.

1/4 pound sliced white bread, crusts removed

1/2 cup heavy cream

2 ounces semisweet chocolate, broken into pieces

1/2 cup butter

1/2 cup ground almonds

3/4 cup caster sugar

4 eggs, each beaten separately

1/2 cup whipping cream

2 tablespoons confectioners sugar, sifted

Well butter a 1 quart mold or dessert bowl. Put the bread into a shallow bowl and pour over the cream. Leave for about 10 minutes, then mash with a fork. Melt the chocolate (page 10). Cream the butter, then, either by hand or using an electric beater, beat in the bread, almonds, sugar and chocolate, and continue beating until the mixture is smooth. Beat in the eggs, one at a time.

Turn the mixture into the prepared mold or bowl. Cover with a double layer of buttered wax paper or with foil, and steam for 1 1/2–2 hours (add more boiling water to the pan if necessary).

Whip the cream until stiff and sweeten with the confectioners sugar. Turn the dessert out of the mold or bowl and serve immediately with the cream.

Serves 6

La Dame Blanche

Found on the menu of every Luxembourg restaurant, this recipe is sometimes made without the meringue shells.

1 cup vanilla ice cream

4 meringue shells

cold Rich Chocolate Sauce (1) (page 89)

CRÈME CHANTILLY

1/2 cup heavy cream

1 egg white

1 tablespoon confectioners sugar, sifted

Make the crème chantilly first. Whip the cream until it holds its shape. Beat the egg white until stiff, then beat in the confectioners sugar, 1 teaspoon at a time. Fold into the cream.

Put two scoops of the ice cream on each serving plate. Top with a meringue shell, then pour over a quarter of the chocolate sauce and top with a quarter of the crème chantilly. Serve at once.

Serves 4

Pots au Chocolat

A wonderful chocolate mousse recipe given to me by a friend in Fife, Scotland. Her pots au chocolat were so popular that she could never give a dinner party without serving them. They also freeze extremely well, so it is worth making a double quantity and freezing half.

1 fat vanilla pod

½ pound semisweet chocolate, broken into pieces

1 tablespoon confectioners sugar

2 tablespoons butter

3 egg yolks

1 cup heavy cream

DECORATION

2 tablespoons flaked almonds

Using a pointed, sharp knife, split open the vanilla pod and, with a small spoon, scrape out all the moist inside. Melt the chocolate, confectioners sugar, butter and the inside of the vanilla pod (page 10). Remove from the heat and beat in the egg yolks. Whip the cream until it holds its shape, then beat in the chocolate mixture and beat until thick. Turn into six small ramekins and sprinkle with the almonds. Chill in a refrigerator until ready to serve.

Serves 6

Saint Emilion au Chocolat

A classic French recipe and a simple way of producing a really elegant dessert.

12–16 macaroons

4 tablespoons dark rum

½ cup butter

¾ cup caster sugar

½ cup milk

1 egg

8 ounces semisweet chocolate, broken into pieces

Put the macaroons on to a serving plate and sprinkle lightly with the rum. Cream together the butter and sugar until light and fluffy. Put the milk into a pan and bring to the boil. Remove from the heat, leave for about 10 minutes to cool, then beat in the egg.

Melt the chocolate (page 10) and, leaving it over the heat, beat in the milk, then the butter and sugar. Continue to beat until very smooth.

Put four of the macaroons into the bottom of a serving bowl. Pour over half the chocolate sauce. Repeat with four more macaroons and the rest of the chocolate sauce. Top with the remaining macaroons. Chill in a refrigerator for at least 12 hours.

Serves 6–8

Chocolate and Pineapple Roulade

A roulade really is the ultimate 'jelly roll' – a cake, but without any flour. I have tried making it both with cocoa and with melted chocolate, and, perhaps surprisingly, prefer a cocoa-based one.

4 eggs, separated

10 tablespoons caster sugar

¼ teaspoon vanilla extract

⅓ cup cocoa powder

FILLING AND DECORATION

1 cup heavy cream

1 pound pineapple pieces, fresh **or** canned and drained

chocolate vermicelli

Grease and line a 13 × 9 inch jelly roll pan. Beat the egg yolks, sugar and vanilla extract until thick and creamy. Beat the egg whites until they form stiff peaks. Fold the cocoa into the egg yolks. Stir in 1 tablespoon of the beaten egg white. Fold in the remainder of the egg white.

Turn the mixture into the prepared pan and spread evenly. Bake in a medium oven, 350°F, for 15 minutes or until just cooked. Do not over-cook or the roll will crack more easily. Remove from the oven, cover with a clean dish towel and leave until quite cold. Invert on to a piece of wax paper dredged with caster sugar, and peel off the paper carefully.

To make the filling, whip the cream until stiff. Reserve a few pieces of the pineapple for decoration and mix the remaining pineapple with two-thirds of the cream. Spread evenly all over the roulade, then roll it up, pushing it along the wax paper. Place on a serving plate. Pipe the remaining cream along the top to decorate, and top with the remaining pieces of pineapple and the chocolate vermicelli.

Serves 6–8

Note *Do not worry if the roulade cracks slightly when you roll it up as you can always mask the cracks with cream or sprinkle confectioners sugar over them.*

Bavarois au Chocolat

Molded desserts were particularly popular during Queen Victoria's reign. A Victorian style china mold will create a truly authentic looking dessert.

1 envelope powdered gelatin

4 tablespoons cold water

4 egg yolks

¼ cup caster sugar

1 teaspoon vanilla extract

2 cups milk

8 ounces semisweet chocolate, broken into small pieces

½ cup heavy cream

½ cup light cream

DECORATION
chocolate curls (page 12) **or** *whipped cream*

Oil a 1½ quart mold lightly or dampen with cold water. Sprinkle the gelatin over the water in a bowl and leave to soften for about 5 minutes. Beat together the egg yolks, sugar and vanilla extract for 5 minutes. Warm the milk and stir into the egg yolks and sugar. Blend well and put into the top of a double boiler, or into a bowl placed over a pan of gently simmering water. Cook gently, stirring all the time, until the mixture thickens. Stir in the softened gelatin and, when this has dissolved, add the chocolate. Stir until the chocolate has melted. Remove from the heat, put into a cold place and leave until the mixture begins to thicken. Whip the light and heavy creams lightly and fold into the mixture when it is thick but not set. Turn into the prepared mold and chill for at least 2 hours or until set.

To turn out, dip the mold into boiling water (see Note). Invert on to a plate and remove the mold. Decorate with chocolate curls or whipped cream.

Serves 6–8

Note *If using a tin mold, dip for 3–4 seconds. If using a china mold, about 15 seconds will be required.*

Index